Facilitating Practitioner Research

Facilitating Practitioner Research: Developing transformational partnerships addresses the complex dilemmas and issues that arise in practitioner inquiry. It recognises that facilitating practitioner research is far more than providing advice about method adoption, important as that contribution is; or even modelling research practices and drawing attention to appropriate resources and theories. It also requires the evolution of strong reciprocal partnerships that will contribute to professional knowledge formation in both the academy and the field.

When such engagement is undertaken then matters associated with authentic 'praxis development' for field-based and academic practitioners emerge. The authors explore:

- how praxis, as practice that can always be judged in terms of 'what is' and 'what ought to be', can be analysed in terms of functional and substantive rationality as well as lifeworld and system issues
- how a transformative partnership requires particular professional attitudes of practitioners and academics
- the underlying potential of practitioner inquiry where agency is afforded as a democratic principle to all who participate, including the consequential stakeholders; the students in our schools and universities.

It draws upon extensive case studies from the Netherlands, Sweden and Australia, which not only illustrate and illuminate, but also highlight contradictions and tensions. The case studies exhibit issues related to the quality of the partnerships between the academy and the field and the ways in which quality impacts upon practice. Additionally, the varying social geographies allow a discussion of different intellectual traditions, belief systems, problem settings, questions and discourses.

Facilitating Practitioner Research: Developing transformational partnerships will appeal internationally to academics involved with practitioner research. It will also prove useful to practitioners across the education sectors, including researchers, teachers and those involved in education policy.

Susan Groundwater-Smith is an Honorary Professor of Education in the Faculty of Education and Social Work at the University of Sydney, Australia

Jane Mitchell is an Associate Professor at the Faculty of Education at Charles Sturt University, Australia

Nicole Mockler is a Senior Lecturer at the School of Education, University of Newcastle, Australia

Petra Ponte was until recently Professor in the Education Research Centre at Utrecht University of Applied Sciences; she is an Honorary Professor of Education at the University of Sydney and an Adjunct Professor at Charles Sturt University, Australia

Karin Rönnerman is a Professor at the Faculty of Education at the University of Gothenburg, Sweden and an Adjunct Professor at Charles Sturt University, Australia

Facilitating Practitioner Research

Developing transformational partnerships

Susan Groundwater-Smith,
Jane Mitchell, Nicole Mockler,
Petra Ponte and
Karin Rönnerman

Routledge
Taylor & Francis Group

LONDON AND NEW YORK

First published 2013
by Routledge
2 Park Square, Milton Park, Abingdon, Oxon OX14 4RN

Simultaneously published in the USA and Canada
by Routledge
711 Third Avenue, New York, NY 10017

Routledge is an imprint of the Taylor & Francis Group, an informa business

© 2013 Susan Groundwater-Smith, Jane Mitchell, Nicole Mockler, Petra Ponte and Karin Rönnerman

The right of Susan Groundwater-Smith, Jane Mitchell, Nicole Mockler, Petra Ponte and Karin Rönnerman to be identified as authors of this work has been asserted by them in accordance with sections 77 and 78 of the Copyright, Designs and Patents Act 1988.

British Library Cataloguing in Publication Data
A catalogue record for this book is available from the British Library

Library of Congress Cataloging in Publication Data
Facilitating practitioner research : developing transformational
    partnerships / Susan Groundwater-Smith... [et al.]
        p. cm.
    ISBN: 978-0-415-68441-5 (hardback) — ISBN: 978-0-415-68442-2
    (paperback) — ISBN: 978-0-203-80317-2 (e-book)   1. Action
    research in education.   2. Education—Research—Methodology.
    I. Groundwater-Smith, Susan.
    LB1028.24.F34 2012
    370.72—dc23

                                                            2012004201

ISBN: 978-0-415-68441-5 (hbk)
ISBN: 978-0-415-68442-2 (pbk)
ISBN: 978-0-203-80317-2 (ebk)

Typeset in Galliard
by RefineCatch Limited, Bungay, Suffolk

MIX
Paper from
responsible sources
FSC
www.fsc.org   FSC® C004839

Printed and bound in Great Britain by
TJ International Ltd, Padstow, Cornwall

Contents

Figures and tables

Figures

Tables

Preface

Writing of aspects of professional practice in terms of procedures, perspectives and underlying philosophy in ways that go beyond mere advice is always a challenging business. How much more interesting and testing the task is when it is shared between five authors, each of whom has her own professional history, social context and language conventions within which her thinking is embedded. This book is a complex discussion of the ways in which those in the academy, functioning in various contexts, can engage in facilitating practitioner research in education such that both the university sector and the field can benefit and contribute to the transformation of practice.

Unlike an edited collection of papers each of the contributors has given voice to the chapters of the book, in particular those introducing the underlying precepts upon which the text is based, the knowledge interests that are served and the ways in which principles and procedures may be mapped into a coherent framework. At the same time each one of the five authors has taken a lead in those chapters based upon case studies arising from her own professional engagement.

In this way co-authoring the book has required a delicate, ongoing and continuous discussion that has laid bare ways in which practitioner research is understood and enacted. The first language of the writers has included English, Swedish and Dutch. While clearly the language of the text is English, this multi-vocal discourse has meant that various linguistic and philosophical dilemmas have needed to be addressed. When struggling with concepts such as 'praxis', different understandings have emerged and been debated. Similarly, the selection of a key word or phrase has required us to ensure that our meaning is clear. An example is where we have chosen to employ the term 'perspective' to develop those attributes and practices that contribute to facilitation that is democratic and liberatory in nature. Originally we had imagined that matters such as substance, sustainability or communicability could be seen as criteria, but quickly came to see that this would provide a signal that each was capable of assessment on a scale of fulfilment. As well, 'criteria' did not sit easily alongside issues in relation to the political environment and notions of teacher professional learning; thus 'perspective' was seen to meet our needs more satisfactorily.

These are no mere quibbles. Furthermore, we see the careful negotiation of the text as a strength of the book in that not only has it required the close and careful attention of the writers, it is also one that makes intellectual demands of its readers. It is a book that is enriched by its extended discussions that go well beyond pragmatic accounts of the academy and field working together. Meaning is revealed in the range of contexts that are discussed.

As a collective of authors we eschew the notion of resorting to the kind of 'newspeak' that characterises so much of contemporary writing in education. 'Newspeak' is the term that was invented by George Orwell in his dystopian novel *1984*, where control is exercised through a language that limits how people may think and act. In explaining 'newspeak' to Winston Smith, the major protagonist in the work, it is said:

> Don't you see that the whole aim of Newspeak is to narrow the range of thought? Has it ever occurred to you, Winston, that by the year 2050, at the very latest, not a single human being will be alive who could understand such a conversation as we are having now? The whole climate of thought will be different. In fact, there will be no thought, as we understand it now. Orthodoxy means not thinking – not needing to think. Orthodoxy is unconsciousness.
>
> (George Orwell, *1984*, Bk 1, Ch. 5)

Rather than use the kind of impoverished, reduced and over-simplified language of those 'how to' works, designed to smooth over the problematics of practice, and requiring some kind of slavish adherence, we have chosen to require of ourselves and of our readers that we collectively render the challenges and difficulties a much greater and intense scrutiny.

It is our collective hope that this publication will contribute to an ongoing and vigorous conversation between those educators working in the academy and those practising in the field, not only in schools but also in organisational structures such as employing authorities and government departments. We write in recognition that there is no single problem when it comes to the support, encouragement and enabling of practitioner research, but rather that there are many intersecting matters to be untangled and addressed.

Chapter I

Introduction

Can it be kindness not to tell what you see and a blessing to be blind. And the best aid to human happiness that has ever been invented is a blanket of soft white lies.

(Swift, 1988, quoted by Cameros, undated)

Graham Swift, Booker Prize winner, defies his readers who elect to look long and hard at the human condition, and aims instead for them to bury themselves under a 'blanket of soft white lies'. It is the intention of this book to take the less comfortable road and pull the covers back on what counts as facilitation of practitioner research within partnership arrangements, how it works and for whom. Such research conducted in partnership, also named as 'action research' and 'teacher inquiry', refers to collaborative knowledge building by practitioners in the university and the field as they together systematically investigate issues and challenges that matter to them. The authors choose to deal with the need to fortify understandings of facilitation that come about as the result of an intense scrutiny of educational work. Such scrutiny can result in constructive practical theorising that directly addresses the dilemmas, tensions and contradictions that are faced daily by practitioners in both schools and universities as they address some of these challenging issues in education. It will argue for a mutually supportive relationship between those in the field and those in academia; a relationship that is generative of new professional knowledge that has the capacity to loosen the ties of unreflective routines. We believe that the text should contribute to the mutually constitutive and potentially transformative nature of developing understandings that can evolve in different and varying sites each with its own constraints and challenges by way of a dialogic enterprise that values but also challenges each participant's experience and knowledge.

Our purpose, then, is to develop a form of practical theorising that allows the emergence of a more nuanced and complex framing of facilitation, taking it beyond the commonplace understanding of providing assistance to the field and moving it into the realm of transformative partnerships between the academy and the field of practice, with all of the challenges and uncertainties that such a relationship entails. We are mindful of the orientation in our work towards the relationship between the academy and school education but claim that those engaged in health and social care will find resonances to their own circumstances.

Facilitating research with practitioners can be all too easily read as a process that is transactional; that is the provision of resources and skills to be handed on from one party to another. We argue instead for a reciprocal relationship that recognises that the boundaries between the actors are of a far more permeable nature than has been hitherto recognised. Mailer, Simich, Jacobson and Wise (2008: 305) define reciprocity as 'an ongoing process of exchange with the aim of establishing and maintaining equality between parties', a definition that serves our purposes well. We see that there is much greater depth and complexity attached to the notion of partnerships, that are currently too readily constructed merely as a combinatorial exercise that can mask status and power asymmetries. We are mindful of the position taken up by Yappa (1998), a cultural geographer, who suggests that the academy views the community as the domain of the problem and the university as the domain of the solution. We see that such a position adopts a deficit model of practice, rather than seeking to recognise professional assets and capacities. We see invention and intervention as available to all who are engaged in an bona-fide professional partnership, while at the same time acknowledging that if partnerships are to be truly transformative then they require what we call in this publication an informed understanding of: substance, politics, sustainability, professional learning and communicability. We will argue in the next chapters that such an understanding of these five perspectives can best be achieved through dialogue and debate.

Thus this is a text that serves to clarify and elucidate the functions of partnership within the context of research with field-based practitioners and to explore the ways in which that research can be facilitated. Its perspective is that of the academic practitioner, which of course is not a singular one, but it also recognises the multiplicity and complexity of roles that are taken by those working in contexts beyond the university. To serve these ends the book is divided into eight chapters: this introduction, which creates the rationale for the book, whose object is to examine the strategies and mores of facilitated practitioner research based within the concept of a mutual transformational relationship. A set of five chapters follow, each of which will specifically focus upon an identified perspective and develop it by using a case study as a form of illumination and to act as a touchstone for discussion. The seventh chapter will attend to matters related to the nature of the facilitation of practitioner research with respect to the development of professional knowledge. Finally, the conclusion will draw together the implications for both academic and teacher professional learning and more broadly, in an international context, a recognition of the substantial contribution made to practice by those working in these varying sites of endeavour.

In writing this book we acknowledge that the contrasting terms 'transactional' and 'transformational' are ones that have been used, in particular, in contexts of leadership discussions. Burns (1978) in his influential work on leadership saw transactional leadership as an exchange process between leaders and followers; it is one that is short term and pragmatic while transformational leadership pays greater attention to a concern for the moral purposes of the enterprise seeking to meet a collective purpose designed to 'produce social change and that will satisfy followers' authentic needs' (p. 4). The coining of the distinction, then, lies with Burns and it may be seen that he has characterised leadership within a leaders/ followers framework. Bass (1990) takes the work further and pleads for the trans-formative leader to transcend the mere 'how' something might be undertaken to explore more closely 'why' it should be done. Stewart (2006) in her discussion of the work of, among others, Burns and Bass draws upon Evers and Lakomski (1996) who argue that leadership, as it is conceptualised in the literature, is not helpful in meeting the challenges of the current educational system. They suggest

> Schools can be thought of as being made up of intricate nets of complex interrelationships that criss-cross formal positions of authority and power and carry knowledge and expertise in all directions, not just downwards as suggested by [transformational] leadership (p. 72).

Furthermore, they posit that transformational models rely too heavily on the transformational skills of the leader; instead, the organisation should develop feedback loops to learn from its mistakes. This certainly accords with the position that we take in relation to partnerships between universities and the field in the facilitation of practitioner research. However, partnerships and organisations have significant differences, for while organisations have established parameters that derive from their purposes, partnerships are more organic and fluid in their nature. We see, therefore, that our discussion is one that reformulates these leadership arguments in the context of democratic partnership, moving from the partner-ships and partnership roles being based upon practical arrangements, important as these are, to ones that can serve an emancipatory function. In this context we eschew the view of the leader in hierarchical terms, preferring a stance where those in the partnership are engaged in an ongoing process of negotiation and re-nego-tiation in the interests of being fair and just to all who participate in the enterprise.

We see that establishing partnerships for the purposes of facilitation is a process that requires thoughtful attention. We believe that the motivations are multiple and may, indeed, be contradictory. Are they formed for legitimation purposes? Are they formed to enable the realisation of goals that have been established by others? Are they formed upon an expectation that a set of practices can be codified and developed as 'one size fits all' solutions? In this chapter we elaborate our motivations as well as our conceptual frameworks. In the chapters that follow we go into those motivations and concepts with particular attention to the ways in which initiatives are taken, the expectations upon which they are based and the sites within which they are developed. More immediately, we wish here to make explicit the theoretical concepts upon which our notion of transformational facilitation rests, namely those associated with praxis.

Facilitation of research in partnerships as praxis

Praxis is the concept we use to critically explore the facilitation of research in transformative partnerships. It is also used to explore the conditions in which these partnerships construct – intersubjectively – practical knowledge about educational practice in the field; these are conditions for participative meaning making, critical dialogue and change. By saying that we use praxis as a concept, we are claiming that knowledge construction in transformative partnerships as well as the facilitation of these partnerships can be seen as social action. We are also claiming that such social action can basically be analysed and criticised in terms of its 'substance' or, in other words, in terms of fundamental normative ideas about what is morally just or unjust. These ideas always have a dialectical relationship with the cultural, social and political contexts in which human beings act. In Chapter 2 we will explore this in depth. In this introduction we present the argument that praxis as a concept for the understanding of moral action always consists of three components: understanding of 'what is' (What is actually happening?); understanding of 'what ought to be' (Where should that lead?) and understanding of how to transform 'what is' into 'what ought to be'. Reflection on these three components is central to the construction of knowledge in transformative partnerships. The aim is to develop a praxis theory that is practical; that is to say a theory that should 'not abstract itself from the intended practice' (Gadotti, 1996), but commit itself to

> educate individuals as a point on the horizon but never a finished process because education is really an unending process . . . Education is at the same time promise and project.
>
> (ibid.: 7)

Many who see the concept of praxis as central to the endeavours of education have drawn upon the wisdom of Aristotle, including: Carr and Kemmis (1986), in their seminal and oft-quoted work *Becoming Critical*; Oancea and Furlong in their discussion of quality criteria in educational research (2008) and Ax and Ponte (2008) whose work is discussed in this section. Bons and Van Ophuijsen (1999) summarise Aristotle's definition of praxis as

> 'action' referring, in a general sense to all intentional activities, by which people can reach a particular goal through their own efforts. More specifically, the term refers to rational action based on a conscious choice . . . and action is defined as the product of observation, desires, and intellect or reason. . . . The inclusion of reason means that action in the narrow sense is the preserve of adults, who are most complete when they are engaged in action and who achieve 'happiness' through action.
>
> (ibid.: 340, translation by the authors)

Aristotle's concept of praxis could be interpreted as psychological. He starts from the premise that human beings are inclined 'to do good' thanks to their natural capacity for reason. Praxis is the purposeful and self-accountable action of the individual who is 'trying to do good' in order to reach happiness. In his view there is also 'non-praxis', that is 'not trying to do good'. Enlightment philosophers in the eighteenth and nineteenth centuries renewed the interest in praxis. In his moral philosophy, however, we see that Kant does not use praxis so much as a psychological but as an epistemological category. He sees praxis as intentional and rational action with which normative judgements should be validated: 'How can I validate this moral claim as just or unjust?' This is deliberative rationality that in his view is obtained through pure reasoning by individuals. Deliberative rationality was reformulated by critical theory in the twentieth century, when praxis became a framework for sociological critique and critical educational theories (Freire, 1972; Gadotti, 1996; Ax and Ponte, 2008; Ponte and Ax, 2009, 2011). As a framework for critique it had major implications for the development of practical theory, and indeed has been highly influential in formulating our understanding of facilitation as a transformative act.

To support our position, we put forward three arguments. First, in contrast to Aristotle's idea that a social situation can be defined as praxis or not praxis, we suggest that every concrete social situation has mores – and so by definition can be critically evaluated through the lens of praxis, no matter what the nature of the action is. According to Gadotti (1996: xvii),

> The kind of education that copies models, that wishes to reproduce models, does not stop being praxis, but is limited to a reiterative, imitative, and bureacratized praxis. Quite different from this, transforming praxis is essentially creative, daring, critical, and reflective.

Second, this critical understanding of praxis as framework supposes deliberative rationality but, unlike Kant, Habermas sees deliberative rationality as obtained by communicative action; the construction of practical theories is not an individual, but an intersubjective endeavour. Third, in understanding the relationship between human action (in our case: facilitation of practitioner research in transformative partnerships) and the cultural, social and political contexts in which human action takes place, praxis does not refer only to individual psychological intentions 'to do good' (as in the Aristotelian definition), but also to social – sometimes unintended, hidden or manipulative – consequences in terms of social equity, justice and solidarity.

The praxis concept offers us a useful framework, therefore, but this still leaves unanswered the question of whether facilitation in research partnerships should be interpreted mainly from the standpoint of practitioners who are capable of acting autonomously and rationally, or mainly from the cultural, social and political contexts in which they act. The first standpoint is represented by lifeworld as seen in the phenomenological theory of Schutz (Schutz and Luckmann, 1989), the second by the system theory of Luhmann (1995). However, our understanding of praxis is strongly inspired by Habermas (1981, 1984, 1987) who tries to overcome this duality. He argues that neither lifeworld theories nor system theories are sufficient to understand social phenomenona. Instead social situations should be interpreted as resulting from the interplay of both forces, and we hold this to be true in relation to the facilitation of practitioner research in transformative partnerships. We develop this viewpoint further in the next section.

Professional scope for autonomous action and rational decision-making

Transformative partnerships in which practical knowledge is construed via participative meaning making, critical dialogue and change assume that professionals do indeed have the opportunity to realise these aims. Those opportunities are determined by two conditions: the scope they are given in educational praxis 1) to act autonomously and 2) to take decisions with regard to the moral aims of their actions. Ax and Ponte (2008: 1–21) – whose line of argument we will follow in the rest of this section – explored this by combining Habermas' concepts of *lifeworld* and *system* with the distinction that Mannheim (1940) (in line with Weber, 1946, first published in 1902–24) made between *functional* and *substantive rationality*. In order to understand their argument, we first look briefly at both theories.

With Habermas' concepts of *lifeworld* and *system* we can problematise the professional scope to act autonomously. *System* in Habermas' theory is the way the world is organised; it has self-regulating dynamics with anonymous mechanisms, on which individuals have little or no influence. *System* is driven by economic, legal, administrative and bureaucratic subsystems. Habermas argues that in modern societies *system* is increasingly uncoupled from its foundations in *lifeworld*, foundations that are necessary for shared sense-making, fair social relationships and mutual solidarity. *Lifeworld* is the domain where people organise their own reality, based on their own preferences and in dialogue with others. *Lifeworld* in current times is increasingly being colonised by *system* in which power and money are the dominant mechanisms, according to Habermas. We see this in education where autonomous scope to act seems to be reduced more and more, under pressure from increasing standardisation and bureaucratisation, handing control over what happens in the school and the university to others (politicians, bureaucrats, etc.). Such colonising clearly has ramifications for practitioner research in transformative partnerships as an emancipatory project (as we will see in Chapter 3 about the politics). This happens, for instance, when practitioner research is appropriated by authorities as an implementation tool or, as Kemmis put it, when 'practitioner research becomes a vehicle for domesticating students and teachers to conventional forms of schooling' (2007: 459).

One of the dangers of colonising *lifeworld* by *system* in neo-liberal times is that moral questions about whose interests various actors in social situations are acting in and where that action should lead to are in danger of no longer being discussed (Ponte and Ax, 2011). This danger requires us to turn to a more finely-tuned distinction with regard to rationality, which is the one that Mannheim (1940), with reference to Weber (1946, first published in 1902–24), makes between *functional rationality* and *substantive rationality*. *Functional rationality* concerns the instrumental decisions about rules, methods, strategies and techniques that are needed to reach a specific goal: of greatest concern in this rationality is the functional usefulness of possible actions. Which instruments do we have at our disposal? Are the measures taken effective and efficient? What works and what does not work? *Substantive rationality*, by contrast, is concerned with the desirability of the actions and the goals to be reached through those actions: of greatest concern in this rationality are the arguments that provide moral legitimacy for an action or the purpose of an action. What are our underlying values? What are our aims? What do these mean for our actual actions? Have we achieved something that is genuinely worthwhile and just?

Professionals must have the necessary degree of say about values and aims, because it is they who ultimately have to reconcile in a professional manner the diverse values and aims of the different stakeholders in education, all of which may be legitimate in themselves (Bull, 1988). This essential power to take decisions about values and aims is the substantive scope for decision-making. Substantive scope is not enough though. Professionals also need functional scope, they need to decide how those values and aims can be realised in practical terms as well. *Substantive* and *functional rationality* are two sides of the same coin. The issue at stake now is that not only are expectations of professionals' *substantive rationality* inflated, so are expectations of their *functional rationality*, and too many policy makers believe that this rationality can also be imposed from outside.

Combining Mannheim's *substantive* and *functional rationality* with Habermas' *system* and *lifeworld* gives us a relevant framework for understanding the professional scope for rational decision-making and autonomous action in transformative research partnerships. This framework is useful for practitioners in both schools and universities and can be represented in a matrix as shown in Figure 1.1 (see Ax and Ponte, 2008: 15).

It is important to emphasise that Ax and Ponte (2008), unlike Habermas (1981, 1984, 1987), Carr and Kemmis (1986) and others, do not equate *system* with *functional rationality* nor *lifeworld* with *substantive rationality*. The relationship between professional rationality and autonomy in education is more complex than that. *System* and *lifeworld* are not strictly partitioned: education is a public enterprise and all of us occupy different positions in both worlds. Moreover, individual responsibility to take substantive and functional decisions exists irrespective of *system* dynamics. This means that educational praxis can be described first and foremost as a reality, meaning that the cells in Figure 1.1 do not represent separate spheres of influence, or a static description of reality, or a prescription of how the educational praxis should be. The cells in Figure 1.1 help us to explore and understand the issues, dilemmas and challenges for transformative partnership with questions such as: To what extent are educational aims prescribed

| | | Scope for autonomous action | |
		System	Lifeworld
Scope for rational decision-making	Substantive rationality	**1** To what extent are educational aims prescribed by *system*? Who actually forms part of that *system*? What is our own role in *system*?	**2** What scope do we have in our *lifeworld* to set our own aims? What opportunities are there to expand that scope and are we using them?
	Functional rationality	**3** To what extent does the *system* determine how we have to achieve the aims and which parts of the *system* make those decisions?	**4** To what extent can we decide on our own rules and working methods? What scope do we have to do this and how can we increase it?

Figure 1.1 Praxis: professional scope for autonomous action and rational decision-making (see Ax and Ponte, 2008: 15).

by *system*? Who actually forms part of *system*? What is our own role in *system*? (cell 1); What scope do we have in *lifeworld* to set our own objectives? What opportunities are there to expand that scope and are we using them? (cell 2); To what extent does the *system* determine how we have to achieve the aims and which parts of the *system* make those decisions? (cell 3); To what extent can we decide on our own rules and working methods? What scope do we have to do this and how can we increase it? (cell 4); How far are the objectives (cells 1 and 2) in harmony with the methods of working? (cells 3 and 4).

Sayings, doings and relatings in praxis

We continue this discussion with the question of how the interplay between the four cells in Figure 1.1 manifests in concrete practices of transformative partnerships. To make these manifestations visible we turn to what Theodore Schatzki (2002: 73) called 'the site of the social', constituting 'doings' and 'sayings' in social practices:

> A practice is a set of doings and sayings. Because these doings and sayings almost always constitute further actions in the contexts in which they are performed, the set of actions that composes a practice is broader than its doings and sayings alone.

Schatzki's notion is further extended with the concept of 'relatings' in the notion of practice architectures formulated by Kemmis (Kemmis and Grootenboer, 2008; Kemmis, 2008). Doings, sayings and relatings accord with the medium of work in physical space (action, or 'doings'), the medium of language in semantic space (discourse, or 'sayings') and the medium of power in the dimension of social space ('relatings'). We therefore see sayings, doings and relatings as an expression of interplay between *lifeworld* and *system*, and *functional* and *rationality*. 'Sayings' are the discourses that prevail in a particular context. These have been shaped culturally across a passage of time. 'Doings' are the actions themselves that have been formed by material and economic forces. 'Relatings' – formed by socio-political forces – are what Kemmis and Grootenboer (2008) set out as the 'moments in unfolding histories of relationships between people and groups as well as in relation to organisations and institutions' (p. 46). With Schatzki, Kemmis (2008) argues further that when 'sayings', 'doings' and 'relatings' become 'sedimented and institutionalised they then function as mediating preconditions for subsequent practice . . . preconditions that pre-form what kinds of practice will be possible' (p. 25), including those that we may desire and those which are constructed for us. He quotes Marx:

> People make their own history, but they do not make it as they please; they do not make it under self-selected circumstances, but under circumstances

existing already, given and transmitted from the past. The tradition of all dead generations weighs like a nightmare on the brains of the living.

(Kemmis, 2008: 25)

This can be taken as a rather dramatic reminder to us that the modern university and the modern school have built upon long-established traditions that can trammel and constrain them. However, there can be no question that we need to move beyond these. This accounts for our strong focus on the following standpoints. First we do not see 'relatings' as an equal component of practice alongside 'doings' and 'sayings'. Instead we see sayings and doings as necessary expressions of the way partners relate to each other and to the context in which they relate. In other words, the sayings and doings of people indicate that different practices relate to one another. Second, we stress that 'sayings', 'doings' and 'relatings' are not only expressions of pre-figured situations. They also express professionals' hope and possibilities for change and for making history. Based on the praxis concept (see Figure 1.1), we can say that practitioners in schools and universities have the possibility *and* the obligation to enlarge their scope for decision-making and autonomous action within the interplay between *lifeworld* and *system* and *functional* and *substantive rationality*. This is in line with what Sachs (2003) calls activist professionalism.

Finally, it remains problematic that facilitation in the form of instrumental knowledge and practice transfer is still the dominant model. This means that learning defiance as espoused by Neiman (2008) requires not only insight and courage, but a profound and deep regard for the moral consequences of our decisions in whatever role we act, or as Kant put it in 1784, 'have courage to use your own understanding'.

Beyond the gap

Following this discussion of praxis and practice architectures, we need now to locate the parties with whom we are concerned, universities and the cognate fields of practice, in terms of their relationship with each other. Is there a gap, a fissure, or an unbridgeable chasm? Do they share an understanding of research and its impact upon practice? Do they propose different approaches and solutions? In order to address this complex and troubling question, we shall turn to the identification, problematisation and actualisation of 'the gap'.

A gap? Yes or no?

By taking the praxis lens in exploring transformative partnerships, we are in line with Rogers (2003: 65), who explored the argument that 'wise and practical ethical and moral judgements are central to an understanding of teachers' daily work' – a stance shared by the authors of this book and which is seen as the interplay between the cells in Figure 1.1. In her article Rogers refutes the notion that for practice to be research informed it should be seen to be following a trajectory that implements the results of [quasi] scientific inquiry. This notion has been the focus of a significant and intensifying discussion regarding the perceived gap between educational research, as it is conducted in universities, and practice, as it is articulated and undertaken in schools. In the discussion it has often been conceptualised as a gap between theory and practice and the discussion is recognised in most countries. For example, the Australian Department of Training and Youth Affairs (DETYA, 2000) published a report, through a series of invited papers, examining the relationship between university-based research and activities related to school education. In the report it was stated that in terms of direct impact 'the most frequently quoted examples of systematic educational enquiry was action research since it appeared to bring immediate benefit' (p. 6). Furthermore the study found that there was a complex space between practitioners and policy makers and what was defined as the 'connecting web' (pp. 342–343). This web was that which links research knowledge, usually generated in the academy, to practitioners' and policy makers' actions through a series of nodes comprising: conferences, professional learning opportunities, taskforces and reference groups, formal meetings, publications, internet sites and the like. It was seen that a powerful node of the web was collaborative research that was capable of joining the thinking and actions of practitioners and policy makers with their academic colleagues. This section of the report concluded that 'there is a real gap between research knowledge and the connecting web: research has to be propelled out of its abstract conceptual space and into arenas where educators can engage with it' (p. 343). What is noteworthy in the analysis is that the gap appears to be in this intermediate space between the academy and the various mediating instruments that could bring the work of the academy to the attention of the schools.

Approaches to the gap

There are many approaches to overcome the gap. Some are instrumental. These approaches are problematised by Ponte (2009) based on information provided to professors from the National Association for Applied Sciences Universities in the Netherlands. In this information, practice-based research is defined in a problem-based sense:

> Practice-based research does not aim to develop theory in the first instance, but to solve practical problems confronting professionals in their work. In practice-based research questions are formulated that stem from practice or

are directly relevant to it. The findings of practice-based research are relevant for the same professional practice and are actively implemented in the practice and in teacher education.

(www.lectoren.nl, translation by the author)

For, while this definition backs up the general idea that the purpose of practice-based research is to contribute to improving professional practice, it stops short of fulfilling the liberatory purpose for which we argue and which is more fully embodied in practitioner research, where those in the field have a greater degree of agency and autonomy. Improving practice is not disputed if it fulfils the ambition of transcending only technical processes linked to the teaching effectiveness movement. So what we ask is that we do not fall into the trap of investing all of our work in a technical response that does not have the potential to take our reflexive thinking about practice further. This does not alter the fact that there are differences of opinion about how the contribution by the academy is being realised and could be realised; in other words how a connection is made between research and education as it is enacted in the field. Is it really always about 'solving problems of professionals in their work'? Is it really always about 'formulating questions that stem from practice or are directly relevant to it'? Is it really always about 'implementing research findings'? What exactly do we mean by that? What alternatives do we have?

Moreover we would argue, the very concept of 'usefulness' is itself contestable. There is an implicit press towards an engineering model; where the research design, development and field-based implementation is driven by expert knowledge that evolves in the academy and is then implemented in the field. Often this was seen through the provision of text book materials, developed by researchers and supported by professional development, that encouraged teachers to teach to a text, embodying a set of procedures, that had been evolved by others (Briars and Resnick, 2000). The model is a linear one that progresses from the research to the practice as noted by Burkhardt and Schoenfeld (2003) who advocate for a process that involves greater reciprocity. Nevertheless, they continue to adhere to principles for change that emanate from the academy, albeit with the proviso:

> We wish to stress that a consensus on findings need not come at the cost of methodological pluralism . . . that as in all science and engineering, there is a wide range of ways of conducting high-quality research in education – and that triangulation using multiple methods is one fundamental way to establish robust findings.

(ibid.: 10–11)

Another approach stems from the late Lawrence Stenhouse who advocated, within the field of education, that teachers evolve a self-critical, purposeful examination of practice for the benefit of both themselves and their students. He concluded his chapter upon Teacher as Researcher in this way:

> It is difficult to see how teaching can be improved or how curriculum proposals can be evaluated without self-monitoring on the part of teachers. A research tradition which is accessible to teachers and which feeds teaching must be created if education is to be significantly improved.
>
> (Stenhouse, 1975: 165)

While Stenhouse advocated for teachers' participation in educational research, he did so on the basis of its capacity to liberate teachers from what were essentially technical constraints. In more recent years the evolution of practitioner research has taken a somewhat different turn. Hargreaves (1996: 7), then Professor of Education at the University of Cambridge, called for an end to the

> frankly second-rate educational research which does not make a serious contribution to fundamental theory or knowledge; which is irrelevant to practice; which is uncoordinated with any preceding or follow-up research; and which clutters up academic journals that virtually nobody reads.

Politicians seized upon the ensuing debate and urged an adoption of 'evidence-based policy and practice' (Clarke 1998: 8). Commissioned reports followed (Hillage, Pearson, Anderson and Tamkin, 1998; Tooley and Darby, 1998). The push was away from academic research toward studies that could be characterised as 'useful' for policy makers and practitioners. In this context practitioner research, particularly in the UK and Australia, took a turn towards addressing those concerns that politicians and their policy advisors had identified as problematic rather than ones that were necessarily of interest or high priority to those in the field (Groundwater-Smith and Mockler, 2009). This scenario was also identified by Carr and Kemmis (2005) as a trap in which action research becomes 'transformed into little more than a research method that could be readily assimilated to and accommodated within the broader requirements of the orthodox research paradigms' (p. 351). Somekh and Zeichner (2009) explore the notion of action research as 'globalization from below' to demonstrate the extent to which action research serves as a localised response to broader global processes.

Dealing with the gap: it's not easy

Many writers have now acknowledged that some kind of fissure exists between the knowledge that educational research, as conducted in the academy, has generated and the practices of school education. Knowledge is commonly divided into two fields: scientific knowledge and practical knowledge. Our daily lives are influenced by both these fields; they are both sources of professional knowledge. McIntyre (2005) has posited that there are several contrasting features between the professional knowledge needs of teachers and the knowledge generated by academic researchers. He argues that research-based propositional knowledge cannot be directly translated into pedagogical knowledge. Teachers are oriented to practicality while researchers are concerned with their obligations to prioritise the clarity and coherence of their arguments and the truth claims that they make. If we think of transformative partnerships as defined in the previous sections (transformative partnerships aim at reflection and transformations), we might find ways to go beyond the characteristics specific to these fields. While there are varying processes and procedures one thing we find agreement upon is that the participation of the field is necessary.

Many will agree that this solution is not as easy as it looks. Lehndals Rosendahl and Rönnerman published an account of an investigation based in Sweden in the *Journal of In-service Education* (Lehndals Rosendahl and Rönnerman, 2006). The focus of the report was specifically upon facilitation and what it meant for teachers, school managers and university researchers. Facilitation had been a process taken up across Sweden as a form of local teacher and school development. Lendahls Rosendahl and Rönnerman argued that while there were expectations that the nexus between facilitators (read academic practitioners) and teachers would be uncomplicated and positive leading to an 'enrichment of learning' (p. 501), a gap such as that discussed earlier in this chapter continues to exist. They saw that facilitation, as a means of bridging the two domains of educational research and teaching practice, requires a closer and more complete investigation. As a result a study was undertaken by means of interviews conducted over a two-month period. Teachers, school managers and academics across four projects were interviewed. It was noteable that the different parties had widely diverging opinions and were unaware of each other's opinions. The emergent categories related to expectations, opinions regarding the legitimacy of the facilitators and opinions regarding processes for establishing mutual understanding. In the case of these expectations, it became clear that teachers hoped for immediate advice in the form of solutions for difficult problems, whereas the facilitators had expected that they might encourage teachers to identify their own capacities for reflection and action. At times, feelings were so strong, that it was seen that expectations were 'entirely contradictory' (p. 503).

Perhaps because they occupied the middle ground the school managers could see the legitimacy of drawing in the academic facilitators. However, the teachers were sceptical, echoing some of the other points made earlier in this chapter. Teachers saw academics as a potential source of new ideas regarding teaching, but facilitators saw that they were charged with offering theoretical tools that the teachers could critique and subsequently employ.

The study argued that mutual understanding first requires the goodwill and capacity to communicate effectively. Procedures for clarifying notions of practice were not sufficiently well embedded in the work practices of any of the parties, thus impeding meaningful dialogue. An important conclusion to the paper was that a more systematic study of facilitation is required that can lead to reciprocal learning and overall educational improvement. In this book we present examples of how professionals are dealing with the gaps and the challenges they are facing.

Dealing with the challenges

In spite of the reservations and concerns that have been expressed thus far, there are good examples of ways in which academics and field-based practitioners have connected successfully, particularly through the processes of partnerships in which academics have worked successfully alongside their colleagues in schools and in classrooms, and these form the core of the chapters that follow. In dealing with challenges Lingard and Renshaw (2010) see teaching as a 'research informed and research informing profession' and teachers as active participants in the research process. They are valued as researchers in their own right. Indeed, they argue for teachers to be generators and utilisers of research within a dynamic construction that recommends that they have a 'researchly disposition' (p. 27). In this book we are especially concerned with foregrounding the ways in which teachers' work and teachers' accounts of their work can be a rich resource for the academy.

Embracing the gap: the contribution of this book

The purpose of this book then is to explore the ways in which transformational facilitation can be exercised and negotiated. Each of Chapters 2 to 6 serves to highlight and illuminate what we have named as specific perspectives that have been identified in uncovering the complex relationship between the academy and field in the professional practice of education. These chapters will consider matters related to the critical issues that are grounded in the research and scholarship, namely substance, politics, sustainability, professional learning and communicability. Each will draw upon an extensive case study, but will also engage in cross-case analysis and discussion.

In Chapter 7, the penultimate chapter, we shall further explore issues regarding knowledge formation and ways in which we might address what has come to be seen as a theory–practice dualism that practitioner research had hoped to resolve (Carr and Kemmis, 2005). It will engage with issues related to the knowledge interests that practitioner research seeks to fulfil, paying particular attention to ethical norms and the nature of moral judgement. We aim in the chapter to dispel the notion that the only knowledge that counts is that constructed in the academy and contribute instead to the argument that legitimate theory building occurs at the intersection of both sites of practice. We pay particular attention to relationships between those engaged in these sites and the ways in which each who participates can act as a knowledge worker in concert with others. Finally we identify the critical issues for partnerships in terms of relationships, facilitation, knowledge construction, dilemmas and challenges in terms of the range of perspectives that have been offered in Chapters 2 to 6.

In our concluding chapter we expand the discussion to incorporate a number of issues related to the ways in which academic support for action research can be understood as more than an implementation tool, more than 'lending a helping hand' but is the crucial interface between two different sites of practice, each deserving respect and recognition. We shall return to the praxis model presented here in Figure 1.1, referring back to Chapters 2 to 6 to elaborate on the notion of transformational partnership developed in and through practitioner research. This results in an overall framework, presented as a lens through which facilitation of practitioner research in transformative partnerships can be analysed, problematised and understood.

References

Ax, J. and Ponte, P. (2008). Praxis: Analysis of theory and practice. In J. Ax and P. Ponte (Eds) *Critiquing praxis* (pp. 1–20). Rotterdam: Sense Publishers.

Bass, B. (1990). From transactional to transformational leadership: Learning to share the vision. *Organizational Dynamics*, *18*(3): 19–31.

Bons, J.A.E. and Van Ophuijsen, J.M. (Eds) (1999). *Aristotoles: Ethica.* (Dutch Translation) Groningen: Historische Uitgeverij.

Briars, D. and Resnick, L. (2000). *Standards, assessments – and what else? The essential elements of standards-based school improvement.* Pittsburgh, PA: University of Pittsburgh.

Bull, B.L. (1988). *The limits of teacher professionalization.* Paper presented to the AERA Annual Meeting, New Orleans.

Burkhardt, H. and Schoenfeld, A. (2003). Improving educational research: Toward a more useful, more influential and better-funded enterprise. *Educational Researcher*, *32*(9): 3–14.

Burns, J.M. (1978). *Leadership.* New York: Harper and Row.

Cameros, C. (undated). *Graham Swift – Biographical notes.* http://biography.jrank.org/ pages/4773/Swift-Graham.html. Accessed 10 April, 2010.

Carr, W. and Kemmis, S. (1986). *Becoming critical: Education, knowledge and action research.* London: Falmer Press.

Carr, W. and Kemmis, S. (2005). Staying critical. *Educational Action Research Journal*, *13*(3): 347–335.

Clarke, C. (1998). Resurrecting educational research to raise standards. *Research Intelligence: British Educational Research Association Newsletter, 66*: 8–9.

DETYA (2000). *The impact of educational research.* www.dest.gov.au/archive/highered/respubs/impact/pdf/impact.pdf Accessed 12 April, 2010.

Evers, C.W. and Lakomski, G. (1996). *Exploring educational administration: Coherentist applications and critical debates.* New York: Elsevier Science.

Freire, P. (1972). *Pedagogy of the oppressed.* London: Penguin.

Gadotti, M. (1996). *Pedagogy of praxis. A dialectical philosophy of education.* New York: State University of New York Press.

Groundwater-Smith, S. and Mockler, N. (2003). *Learning to listen: Listening to learn.* Sydney: University of Sydney Faculty of Education & Social Work/MLC School.

Habermas, J. (1981). *Theorie des kommunikatieven Handelns.* Frankfurt am Main: Suhrkamp Verlag.

Habermas, J. (1984). *Theory of communicative action, Volume 1: Reason and the rationalisation of society.* T. McCarthy, Trans. Boston: Beacon Press.

Habermas, J. (1987). *Theory of communicative action, Volume 2: Lifeworld and system: A critique of functionalist reason.* T. McCarthy, Trans. Boston: Beacon Press.

Hargreaves, D. (1996). *Teaching as a research-based profession: Possibilities and prospects.* Teacher Training Agency (TTA) Annual Lecture. London: Teacher Training Agency.

Hillage, J., Pearson, R., Anderson, A. and Tamkin, P. (1998). *Excellence in research on schools.* DfEE Report No. 74. London: Department for Education and Employment.

Kant, I. (1784). *An answer to the question: What is enlightenment?* www.english.upenn. edu/~mgamer/Etexts/kant.html Accessed 5 July, 2011.

Kemmis, S. (2000). *Educational research and evaluation: Opening communicative space.* The 2000 Radford Lecture presented at the Annual Conference of the Australian Association for Research in Education. Sydney: University of Sydney, 5 December.

Kemmis, S. (2007). Participatory action research and the public sphere. In P. Ponte and B.H.J. Smit (Eds) *The quality of practitoner research. Reflections on the position of the researcher and the researched* (pp. 9–29). Rotterdam: Sense Publishers.

Kemmis, S. (2008). *Researching for praxis: Knowing doing.* Paper presented at the Researching Practice conference sponsored by the journal *Pedagogy, Culture and Society* and Gothenburg University. 13 September, 2008.

Kemmis, S. and Grootenboer, P. (2008). Situating praxis in practice: Practice architectures and the cultural, social and material conditions for practice. In S. Kemmis and T. Smith (Eds) *Enabling praxis: Challenges for education* (pp. 37–64). Rotterdam: Sense.

Lehndals Rosendahl, B. and Rönnerman, K. (2006). Facilitating school improvement. *Journal of In-Service Education, 32*(4): 497–509.

Lingard, B. and Renshaw, P. (2010). Teaching as a research-informed and research-informing profession. In A. Campbell and S. Groundwater-Smith (Eds) *Connecting inquiry and professional learning in education: Joining the dots* (pp. 26–39). London: Routledge.

Luhmann, N. (1995). *Social systems.* San Francisco: Stanford University Press.

McIntyre, D. (2005). Bridging the gap between research and practice. *Cambridge Journal of Education*, *35*(3): 357–382.

Mailer, S., Simich, L., Jacobson, N. and Wise, J. (2008). Reciprocity: An ethic for community based participatory actions research. *Action Research*, September 6 (3): 305–325.

Mannheim, K. (1940). *Man and society in an age of reconstruction: Studies in modern social structure*. London: Routledge & Kegan Paul.

Neiman, S. (2008). *Moral clarity: A guide for grown-up idealists*. New York: Harcourt.

NSW DET (2006). *School is for me: Pathways to student engagement*. Sydney: NSW Department of Education and Training. Copies are accessible through the Resources section of the Priority Schools Program PSP website www.psp.nsw.edu.au Accessed 14 April, 2010.

Oancea, A. and Furlong, J. (2008). Expressions of excellence and the assessment of applied and practice-based research. In J. Furlong and A. Oancea (Eds) *Assessing quality in applied and practice-based research in education: Continuing the debate*. London: Routledge.

Ponte, P. (2009). Gedrag en onderzoek in de educatieve praxis: Plaatsbepaling. [Behavior and research in educational praxis: An orientation.] Inaugural speech (Dutch and English verson www.educatie.onderzoek.hu.nl/Data/Press/gedrag-en-onderzoek-in-de-educatieve-praxis, accessed 1 June 2012).

Ponte, P. and Ax, J. (2009). Action research and pedagogy as science of the child's upbringing. In S. Noffke and B. Somekh (Eds) *The Sage handbook of educational action research* (pp. 324–335). London: Sage Publications.

Ponte, P. and Ax, J. (2011). Inquiry-based professional learning in educational praxis: Knowing why, what and how. In N. Mockler and J. Sachs (Eds) *Rethinking educational practice through reflexive inquiry* (p. 49–61). Dordrecht: Springer.

Rogers, B. (2003). Educational research for professional practice: More than providing evidence for doing 'x' rather than 'y' or finding the size of the effect of A on B. *The Australian Educational Researcher*, *30*(2): 65–86.

Sachs, J. (2003). *The activist teaching profession*. Buckingham: Open University Press.

Schatzki, T. (2002). *The site of the social*. University Park PA: Pennsylvania University Press.

Schutz, A. and Luckmann, T. (1973 c1989). *The structures of the life-world (Volume 2)*. Evanston, Illinois: Northwestern University Studies in Phenomenology and Existential Philosophy.

Somekh, B. and Zeichner, K. (2009). Action research for educational reform: Remodelling action research theories and practices in local contexts. *Educational Action Research*, *17*(1): 5–21.

Stenhouse, L. (1975). *An introduction to curriculum research and development*. London: Heinemann Educational Books Ltd.

Stenhouse, L. (1981). What counts as research? *British Journal of Educational Studies*, *29*: 103–114.

Stewart, J. (2006). Transformational leadership: An evolving concept examined through the works of Burns, Bass, Avolio, and Leithwood. *Canadian Journal of Educational Administration and Policy*, Issue #54, June 26 http://umanitoba.ca/publications/cjeap/pdf_files/stewart.pdf Accessed 29 September, 2010.

Swift, G. (1988). *Out of this world*. London: Viking Press.

Tooley, J. and Darby, D. (1998). *Educational research – a critique*. Ofsted report. London: Office for Standards in Education.

Weber, M. (1946 translation). *From Max Weber: Essays in sociology* (Hans H. Gerth and C. Wright Mills, Eds). New York: Oxford University Press (first published in 1906–24).

Yappa, L. (1998). The poverty discourse and the poor in Sri Lanka. *Transactions of the Institute of British Geographers, 23*(1): 95–115.

Chapter 2

Substance

Petra Ponte, who initiated the international Action Research in Teacher Education (ARTE) project, is the lead author of this chapter. ARTE was carried out in close collaboration with researchers, teacher educators and teachers from the Netherlands, Russia, the United Kingdom and the United States. In this chapter, the Dutch element of the project is used to illustrate substantive issues that are inevitable for the facilitation of partnerships that aim to transform educational practices. Substance refers to normative, moral ideas that are continuously at stake in the work that we think should be done. We argue that substantive claims have to be justified by public deliberation, which can be seen as one of the main aims of transformative research partnerships. In ARTE this idea led to facilitation as a kind of hospitality.

Introduction

This chapter will provide a philosophical and practical base for the substantive issues of practitioner research in transformative partnerships and the facilitation of these partnerships. The terms 'substance' and 'substantive' are derived from the Latin '*sub*', which means 'under' and '*stare*', which means 'stand'; so substance is 'that which stands under'. In philosophy these terms refer to moral fundaments of social practices. In philosophy of law, for instance, substance refers to the rules of 'right' that courts are called on to apply, as distinguished from rules of 'procedure'. Parallel to this we can say that for research in transformative partnerships substance refers to the rules of justice (right) that professionals are called on to apply, as distinguished from the rules of method (procedure) they are asked to follow. We also make substantive claims in this publication. After all – as we stated in Chapter 1 – we, the authors of this book, are striving for a world that will make a difference to young people and we are striving for liberated democratic practice. We assume that these claims can be put into practice and justified through practical reasoning and action research in transformative partnerships.

The Dutch element of ARTE is an example of such a partnership (Ponte, 2002a, 2002b; Ponte, Ax, Beijaard and Verloop, 2004). The project involved seven groups of about five teachers carrying out action research over a two-year period. Their research was part of an in-service programme. Each group was facilitated by one of the educators from the participating universities. Educators investigated their own thinking and actions and formed a partnership with me as the academic researcher in order to answer the overall question of the project, which was how teachers learn to do action research and how they can be facilitated to carry it out. The aim of ARTE, therefore, was to develop understanding and to bring about educative change in practice on three levels: teacher, teacher educator and academic researcher. The way the ARTE groups gradually developed can be described – in retrospect – as transformative partnerships because of the following missions.

- *The educative mission*: striving for emancipation for the most vulnerable students via a whole-school programme for student counselling and pastoral care.
- *The professional mission*: striving for empowerment of the teachers who were encouraged to take informal leadership roles in their practitioner research projects and beyond.
- *The research mission*: emphasising the agency role for the people involved in the university as well as in the schools, including students' voice.
- *Structural mission*: establishing conditions for participative decision-making and critical dialogue.
- *The cultural mission*: setting a respectful tone for interaction with those involved in the research and demonstrating a willingness to change practice in the light of new understanding) (see also Karstanje, 2007: 121–123; Mertens, 2009: 1–4).

The study not only had an impact upon inquiry-based practice and the knowledge, skills and actions that are required to more carefully consider practice in terms of teaching; it also had an impact upon the ways in which it led the university facilitators to investigate and transform their thinking and actions. One teacher educator in ARTE said for instance:

> The questions teachers ask themselves (such as: What is my opinion and how did I actually arrive at that opinion? Is this change really an improvement and for whom is it an improvement?), I now ask myself far more than I used to. Teachers have also learned to see pupils as partners and a source of information and I have started to do that too with my students.
>
> (Ponte, 2002a: 399)

The results of the study led to the conclusion that facilitation needs to be more focused on knowledge about substantive dilemmas in complex contexts and therefore that it needs to switch from a rule-based concept to a principle-led concept of action research. This conclusion was inspired by the fact that the ARTE missions are not based on any objective truths, but on substantive claims about the aims and methods of action research. These claims are congruent with 'that which stands under' action research, since Dewey (1929/1930) formulated his democratic ideas about research by and with the field instead of research on the field. These ideas are morally informed; they are not objective but normative, and they are not accidental but continuously at stake in the work that we think should be done in transformative partnerships.

It is our impression, however, that reports on research rarely make substantive claims explicit or define them as problems through thoughtful and critical testing of 'that which stands under' the work done. Action research reports also often fail to address substantive claims or they are simply accepted as given. For instance, sometimes there are only sentimental accounts about the collaboration between the stakeholders in partnerships ('We got on well together and we appreciated the process'), sometimes there are only instrumental accounts ('We made sure that we stuck to the methodological rules and we valued the procedures'). In the first case the substantive claims are ignored and in the second case they are not taken up as research problems. Both risk action research being robbed of its transformative potency, because no-one questions the accepted wisdom. This could result in many descriptions remaining limited to instrumental or celebratory accounts.

This chapter explores the need to discuss accepted wisdom and to focus on substance in transformative research partnerships and in their facilitation. The next section looks at the epistemological background to substance in research, followed by the question of how substance can be justified in partnerships. Then the facilitation of research in transformative partnerships as hospitality is discussed. In the final section a connection is made with praxis as the interplay between *lifeworld* and *system*, and *functional* and *substantive rationality* as explored in Chapter 1.

Epistemological background to substance in transformative research partnerships

It could be argued that action research in ARTE is by definition practice-based, because of the desire to understand and improve educational practice. It could also be argued that with the desire to transform practice, reflection on the substance of practitioner research is inevitable: What should our students learn, for what purpose and from whom? What kind of adults do we want our students to become? For what kind of society are we educating our students? What ethics are at stake as we try to realise our aims? However, there are many different ideas about the role these substantive issues should play in research. We will look at these ideas now.

Value-free, value clarification, value-bound

The answer to what role substance should play in research depends on explicit and implicit assumptions about the nature of the social phenomena that are being investigated (Ponte, 2010). Can human behaviour be compared with the physical world and is it therefore possible to know about it objectively by adopting a scientific approach? This means using approaches arising from the positivism of Compte, which over time have developed into the empirical–analytical science that we know today. Although this science differs on many points from Compte's original ideas, it is still characterised by the search for causality (explaining and predicting) and the reductionism that goes with it. In education this approach has mainly been directed at the desire to contribute to solving practical problems through the development and transfer of instrumental and usable knowledge that is value-free; free therefore from substantive claims and moral judgements. This has led to an emphasis on the question of what interventions are effective, in other words 'what works'. Several scholars have criticised this emphasis on 'what works' (Atkinson, 2000; Blackmore, 2002). Biesta (2007), for instance, calls this a causal model for professional action, a model that he believes is too limited for the following two reasons.

1   If teaching is to have any effect on learning, it is because of the fact that students interpret and try to make sense of what they are being taught. It is only through processes of (mutual) interpretation that education is possible (p. 8).

2   Even if we were able to identify the most effective way of achieving a partic-ular end, we might still decide not to act accordingly . . . . Knowledge about the effectiveness of interventions is not, as such, a sufficient basis for deci-sions about educational action. There is always the question as to whether particular interventions are desirable (p. 9).

Biesta counterposes this with a morally-informed model for professional action. This model conceives the teacher's core task as being to judge what in educative terms is desirable with regard to outcomes as well as processes (Biesta, 2010a and b).

Biesta's argument is in line with Dilthey (1914) who, with the rise of the humanities in the nineteenth century, was arguing that human behaviour is intentional and that reality is therefore largely constructed by human beings themselves. That reality can be understood by exploring and understanding how human beings ascribe meaning to it. As time went by Dilthey's ideas developed into the interpretive approach, which studies questions around human action. These are issues that are not so much about the application of external rules, but mainly concern intentional actions of the people involved and the consequences of those actions whether intentional or not. Educational studies can therefore be defined as the science of 'knowing to act' and the object of study as praxis (Ponte, 2009; Ax and Ponte, 2010; Ponte and Ax, 2011). Praxis – as we defined in Chapter 1 – is a social situation in which the following components are present: how people think that practice 'ought to be' (*substantive rationality*), how education practice 'is', and how to move from 'what is' towards 'what ought to be' (*functional rationality*). The relationship between these components is the essence of education: we know that pupils are at school to become what they not yet are in the here and now. They are at school, according to Biesta (2010a and b), to learn something, to learn something worthwhile and to learn from someone.

An essential aspect of this definition of the research object is that the substantive decision about 'the desirable but not yet existing' (for example, greater pupil participation) cannot be derived logically from 'what is' (no pupil participation) (Ponte, 2010). The empirically established absence of participation does not, after all, tell us anything about the desirability of participation. Deciding that it would be good to allow pupils to participate more and especially deciding what purpose that would serve, how they should participate and the extent to which they should participate are normative decisions. The researcher cannot establish that normative 'reality' objectively, detached from the human being whose intentionality constitutes that reality, thus detached from the human being who ascribes a particular meaning to participation and labels it desirable.

In other words, we can predict that the earth is round and seasons will continue to change until the end of time based on universal laws, regardless of the presence or absence of human beings, regardless of the significance that they ascribe to these phenomena and regardless also of the meaning ascribed to them by the researcher. Praxis, on the other hand, is not a constant that can be established objectively and localised entirely outside the researcher, as is the case with the seasons. Praxis does not exist in the absence of human beings and researchers can only develop knowledge about praxis by understanding the meaning that people give to it (a mountain is a mountain, but for people it can be a step on the way, a phenomenon to enjoy, a thing to climb). Moreover, the researcher him/herself is no objective observer outside that social reality: 'Das Ding an sich dass kennt man nicht', as Kant put it. By that he meant that reality can only be understood through certain categories of knowledge that the researcher has at his or her disposal. Meanwhile we have learned that those categories of knowledge are not so much determined by objective or genetic factors but rather by intersubjective and cultural factors. With the knowledge categories available to them, researchers are part of the social reality that they are studying and, therefore, cannot in fact be addressed as an object–subject relationship, but – as Dilthey put it – a subject–subject relationship. Of course, this is not about intuitive and subjective meanings in the sense of 'What do I personally feel or think about it?', but about the epistemological focus with which reality is examined. What it is really about is the realisation that, for human beings, the possibility of knowing the social world objectively is limited or, as Rousseau (in Neiman, 2008: 249) had already claimed:

> We know the first point from which each of us starts in order to get to the common level of understanding. But who knows the outer limit? I know of no philosopher who has yet been so bold as to say: this is the limit of what man can attain and beyond which he cannot go. We do not know what our nature permits us to be.

It is important to distinguish two broad research approaches within interpretive science: the Geisteswissenschaftliche and the critical approaches (Ponte, 2009). Both criticise the value-free claim of empirical–analytical research. Geisteswissenschaftliche research is not value-free but focuses on clarification of values, that is on investigating substantive claims in real-life situations and informing practice by describing these real-life situations. Action research approaches, however, are not only focused on clarification of values. They are value-bound, because they are based on a priori claims for social change (for social justice) and because they aim to actually transform professional practice on the basis of those claims. Such value-bound research could only take place in collaboration with all those who are involved in the practices to be changed.

In the Dutch element of the ARTE project, I drew the following conclusion:

> If I want to answer the overall question of my research (how teachers learn to do action research and how educators learn to facilitate them), I have to facilitate the teacher educators to do their action research while at the same time they are facilitating the action research of the teachers in the schools. After all, neither the teacher educators nor the teachers with whom I am working in this project are familiar with action research.

Substance and three areas of knowledge

A framework was developed in the course of ARTE that would help understanding of knowledge construction on the three levels of the project (teachers, teacher educators and academic researchers). The framework is based on the theory of Riedel (1977) and – in retrospect – can be reinterpreted here as a nuancing of *substantive* and *functional rationality* as is explained in Chapter 1.

Riedel (1977) distinguished three areas in which knowledge should be developed by the academy, namely the ideological, technological and empirical areas of knowledge. By analogy it could be assumed that practitioners who are carrying out action research should also develop knowledge in these areas themselves. The ideological and technical areas of knowledge both involve knowledge that exists without real action. The ideological domain of knowledge parallels *substantive rationality* and can be summarised as follows:

- The ideological area of knowledge covers the teachers' understanding of norms and values and the objectives based on those norms and values that they want to realise with their pupils. It is therefore concerned with the 'desired impacts and effects' of their teaching: impacts and effects that they plan to realise but have not realised yet.

The technological domain of knowledge parallels *functional rationality* and can be summarised as follows:

- The technological area of knowledge covers the teachers' understanding of methods and strategies that they want to use to realise the objectives they have formulated. This means that it is concerned with 'desired phenomena' of their teaching: phenomena they plan to realise but have not realised yet.

It is important to note now that, based on Riedel, a third area of knowledge can be distinguished, namely the empirical area. This pertains to knowledge about real impacts and effects (i.e. those which have occurred in practice) in relation to real methods and strategies (i.e. those which have been realised in practice). This can be summarised as follows:

- The empirical area of knowledge covers the teachers' understanding of educational reality. It is concerned with the relationship between 'real phenomena' and 'real impacts and effects' in their actual teaching.

These three areas of knowledge will always be integrated into the concrete research activities in transformative partnerships, so a distinction can only be made between the ideological, empirical and technological areas in a formal sense (Riedel, 1977). I can illustrate this with the following example.

In a discussion with teachers, one of the teacher educators (Facilitator Ed) in ARTE referred to desired aims and impacts (*ideological knowledge*): 'You wanted to encourage students to take more initiatives themselves and to ask questions. You used the term "inquisitive questioning" by students.' Then he asked about the relation between actual aims and impacts, and actual actions (*empirical knowledge*): 'You used a survey to get the students' views. Can you briefly say what this exploration produced?' A discussion developed about the interpretation of the data:

Teacher Ann:	The students see independence as 'doing it on your own'. Only a few mention 'asking questions' as well. For most of them working independently means working individually. 'Asking questions' is not part of that and neither is 'taking the initiative'. Just 'picking up your book or your own work'.
Facilitator Ed:	So if you are working on your own that means you are working independently. And if you link this to your idea about the problem? Is this the opposite of what you expected?
Teacher Ann:	I did not expect this.
Teacher Ben:	One of the things you said was that students are often more independent than many teachers think. That was one of your assumptions.
Teacher Ann:	That may be true, but it is not what we mean by working independently, it is not what we want.
Teacher Caroline:	They don't associate working in groups with working independently.
Facilitator Ed:	How do you think they arrived at that view?
Teacher Ann:	As I understand it, they learned it in the past. Keep your mouth shut and get on with your own work.

Finally, the facilitator asked about desired actions (*technical knowledge*): What could you do in response to what you have learned from this exploration?

In addition, he asked about desired aims and impacts (*ideological knowledge*): What do you want to achieve now with your approach? What are your aims?

The collaborative design of the ARTE research allowed me to follow the process closely for over two years. At the same time I was able to discuss and adjust the knowledge construction in the course of the project with the participants. This is what we have learned.

Generally speaking, both teachers and teacher educators tended to go through phases in the emphasis they placed on the areas of knowledge. At first they focused mainly on the technical area of knowledge (What actions are we planning to do?), and after that in turn on the ideological area of knowledge (What kind of impact and effects are we aiming for?) and the empirical area of knowledge (What are our actions actually and how does that relate to the actual impact and effects of our actions?). What stands out here therefore is that left to themselves the participants mainly reflected on desirable and actual actions, and not so much on desirable and actual aims and impacts. In the course of the two-year programme their reflections did tend to broaden in scope, but the fact remains that they only showed a proportional interest in all three areas of knowledge simultaneously if they were explicitly challenged to do so. Another thing that stands out is that there was a kind of 'domino effect'. Teacher educators emphasised all three areas of knowledge at the same time more frequently, the more I as the academic facilitator challenged them to do so. Subsequently, the teachers for their part emphasised all three areas of knowledge at the same time more frequently, the more the teacher educators challenged them to do so. Finally they also challenged each other. The guiding questions I developed as the academic facilitator turned out to be essential to this. These guiding questions were based on the shared experiences in the first phase of the ARTE project, for example:

- *Vision* – What missions, aims and visions do I hold and where can they be placed within the missions, aims and visions of others (the school, colleagues, government, academic research)?
- *Evidence* – How do I know whether my assumptions about a practice (in this case my actions in relation to pupils, colleagues and others) are correct and how do I know whether my actions in this situation will have the desired impact?
- *Dialogue* – How can I involve pupils, colleagues and others in planning, implementing and evaluating my missions, aims, visions and actions?
- *Improvement* – Why do I think that a change is also an improvement and for whom is the change an improvement?
- *Ethics* – Is what I am doing or want to do ethically responsible and, if not, what can I do about that?

A teacher educator initially reported:

> For me at first the guiding questions were so theoretical that I thought: I can't bother teachers with them. But to be fair, I have not made a habit of using the guiding questions myself. That's because I am very practice-oriented: I want to do things not label them. Of course, I'm a bit guilty of double standards there because I do want teachers to do that. I'm looking now at how I can use the guiding questions myself.

Later he admitted:

> It's funny that the guiding questions gradually turned out to be very important, while I hardly mentioned them in my research diary. So perhaps it is

something that just happens as an integral part of what you are doing. All the same I'd like to put it down in writing more.

Foundation for transformation through research

So far it has been argued that action research approaches are value-bound, because they are based on a priori claims for social change and because they aim to actually transform professional practice on the basis of those claims. The foundation for transformation through research in partnerships like ARTE was laid by Dewey (1929/1930) in the twentieth century. He realised how little the psychological laboratory research of his day had to offer teachers and pupils in schools. He sought ways to broaden their horizons and to give them a say in their own actions. He was the first to plead for a multidisciplinary and pluralistic approach, in which laboratory researchers, field researchers, teacher-researchers and pupil-researchers form a community of equal partners. This community should generate knowledge democratically while at the same time contributing to the achievement of democratic education. Even pupils are given a research role. Dewey believed that this was all possible without loss of scientific quality by training researchers in professional skills and training professionals in research skills. Following in Dewey's footsteps, Lewin (1947) developed Dewey's ideas further into a methodology for action research. He created real-life experiments where the people involved (these included women and Jewish minority groups) acted together to try to improve their situation. Lewin conducted these real-life experiments by allowing the people involved to participate as researchers in their own situations. The assumption was that any group that is involved in the situation to be changed should also be involved in the planning and execution of the research and in evaluating the research findings. Lewin proved with his research that participation through democratic group processes in research settings could contribute to successful social action and at the same time contribute to a better scientific understanding of how to solve social problems (Barone, Maddux and Snyder, 1997).

Unfortunately in some continental European countries, Lewin's ideas about action research were linked with dogmatic Marxism and after the 1970s were banished under the influence of the dominant neo-liberal ideas in academia at that time (see Ponte and Rönnerman, 2009). Action research however was again 'imported' from the English-speaking countries, where Lewin's ideas were linked by Stenhouse (1975) to his Teacher-as-Researcher approach. This was further developed in the work of Elliott (1991) in the United Kingdom, Carr and Kemmis (1986) in Australia and Zeichner and Liston (1986) in the United States as a strategy for a morally informed model for professional practice. Nevertheless this research approach is still under threat because of the dominant one-sided, neo-liberal rhetoric about objectivity in social theory and evidence-based practice in education. According to Neiman (2008), we live in an age in which moral claims make many of us feel profoundly uncomfortable. If they are made at all, such claims

> are subject to quotation marks – sometimes called scare quotes – that express the speaker's discomfort in the ultimate postmodern gesture, fingers wiggling beside ears in a little dance that says: I can use it, but I don't go so far as to mean it, and it all matters so little anyway I can make myself look silly to boot. What matters is putting distance between you and your beliefs (p. 18).

Substance needs to be justified

The discomfort to which Neiman is referring leads to the central question for research in transformative partnerships about how substantive claims can be justified and validated. In the previous section we established that these substantive claims cannot be justified on the basis of pure empiricism: our professional action is not by definition just simply because that is the way it is. Nor can intuition alone be the basis for justification: our professional action is not by definition just simply because we feel that something is good. A third possibility, that is justification of substantive judgements based on external people in authority, would be a contradiction in terms. Our professional claims are not by definition just because we are following instructions from the church, state, science or other institutions. After all, research in transformative partnerships is about participants forming autonomous and critical judgements. Substantive judgements by external institutions can inspire and inform but nothing is by definition just simply because another says that it is. As we have seen, this was also the viewpoint of Dewey, Lewin and later scholars in the field of action research. Below we argue that their position naturally leads on to the assumption that substantive statements must be justified through deliberative practical rationality. First the theories of Kant and Habermas are explored, then these theories are further elaborated with the 'Expressive elaboration model' of Gilabert (2005a and b, 2006).

Deliberative practical rationality

Theories about deliberative practical rationality claim that the rightness of moral judgements depends on their being rationally justifiable to all those affected in the practice of public deliberation (Gilabert, 2005b). The basis for this argument was laid in the Enlightenment philosophy of Kant. It was Habermas who reformulated this philosophy into the theory of communicative action, a theory that has played an important role in the debate on action research (Carr and Kemmis, 1986).

Central to Kant's moral theory (1999, edited by Wood and Guyer) are the categorical imperative and the test of universalisability. Simply put, the categorical imperative means that people should act in the way they would want everyone to act. Then the categorical imperative must be able to stand the test of universalisability. This test is based on the assumption that only those principles 'which all rational beings could accept for the same reasons' are valid (Gilabert, 2005a: 407). It consists of three steps: 1) taking a maxim, which includes the description of an action and its immediate motives; 2) considering whether that maxim is universalisable (Could I will that everyone do what I seem to want to do?) and 3) taking the action presented by the maxim as an obligation, a permission or a prohibition. According to Gilabert, whose line of argument we follow in the rest of this section and partly summarise (see Gilabert, 2005a and b, 2006), Habermas's theory of communicative action (1981) reformulates Kant's moral philosophy in a number of important respects. The essence – insofar as it is relevant to our point – can be summarised as follows.

First of all Kant makes a rigorous distinction between substantive issues of justice (which he calls morality) and practical issues of the good life (which he calls ethics). Morality is concerned with statements about how we ought to treat each other in a just society. Ethics is concerned with statements and advice about the good life. Habermas develops this distinction further but is less strict about it than Kant. He takes the view that statements about the good life can indeed have a role in the formulation of substantive judgements. This is conditional upon the good life being evaluated in the light of its impact on the interests of all; that is in the light of human beings' duties toward one another. Secondly, with the distinction between justice and the good life Kant wanted to de-privatise moral principles. Justifying justice through rational argument, according to him, belongs to the domain of practical knowledge construction. Habermas endorsed this, but unlike Kant argued that the knowledge of what is just cannot be entirely separated from inclinations, motives and interests. Finally, Kant conceived the universality of substantive statements as the outcome of the formal procedure for rational argumentation. Habermas does that too, but unlike Kant he does not take the universalisation procedure to be something to run introspectively by any individual subject in isolation. Habermas sees deliberative practical rationality as an intersubjective practice – via public deliberation – in which according to Gilabert (2006: 215):

> people select and ground the rules that are given to govern their common life with regard to issues of justice . . . The norms justified in such practice,

as well as their application, are to be determined by argumentative processes in which all those concerned can participate.

The outcome must be equally in the interest of all. According to Habermas (1981), not only pure reason but also moral intentions and consequences must play a role in this procedure. Carr and Kemmis (1986, see also Kemmis, 2001; Kemmis and Grootenboer, 2008) used Habermas's theory as a firm foundation for participatory action research (PAR). They define PAR as:

> a form of self-reflective inquiry undertaken by participants in social situations in order to improve the rationality and justice of their own social or educational practices, their understanding of these practices, and the situation in which the practices are carried out (Carr and Kemmis, 1986: 162).

Expressive elaboration model

At the heart of the approach of Carr and Kemmis (1986) are the rules for 'communicative action' and 'the ideal speech situation' borrowed from Habermas, which should be followed in order to justify substantive judgements. Chapters 4, 5 and 6 examine this in more depth. Here it is important that – in moral philosophical terms – ideas about communicative action and the ideal speech situation mirror a proceduralistic approach; justification is after all based on intersubjective practices of 'giving and asking for practical reasons with help from certain guidelines'. Many moral philosophers believe that such a proceduralistic approach can lead to empty formalism, purely directed at *functional rationality* and pragmatic problem-solving (Gilabert, 2005a and b, 2006; Neiman, 2008). For Gilabert (2005a and b, 2006) these concerns were reason to propose an 'expressive elaboration model' based on a substantivist construal of Habermas's deliberative practical rationality. In his model he argues that procedure and substance cannot do without each other: procedure is coloured by substance and claiming substance is not possible without procedure. In other words: deliberative rationality is a practical medium in which basic substantive ideas of social justice are expressed and elaborated. For this reason he breaks his model down into three levels of substance (2005b: 187):

- *First order*: specific ethical norms placing constraints on how to apply basic moral ideas in practice.
- *Second order*: norms determining the practices of decision-making and justification concerning the first order norms.
- *Third order*: basic moral ideas as the foundation for social justice.

Gilabert equates third order substance with the Enlightenment ideals of freedom, equality and solidarity; ideals established in the French Revolution and elsewhere. These ideals are the source of human rights and social justice, and are therefore also the source of democratic and emancipatory forms of research. The third order ideals are expressed first in second order substance, that is in the procedural form of deliberation itself. In our case we could even go so far as to say that these ideals have already been expressed in the very fact that action reseach in partnerships – as a form of public deliberative and practical rationality – was invented, including its dialogical rules. Second, they are elaborated in the selection of topics and outcomes of deliberation, whereby the general substantive ideas are interpreted and applied to specific situations. This line of reasoning leads, according to Gilabert (2005a and b, 2006), to two dimensions of substantive expression and elaboration:

- *Expression*: the substantive ideas as being resources expressed by deliberative procedure.
- *Elaboration*: the substantive ideas as being results of their elaboration by use of the deliberative procedure.

Gilabert (2005b: 198) then justifies his proposal by posing two questions:

> Would one endorse the three substantive ideas without being normatively moved by what deliberative practical rationality demands and, vice versa, would one be committed to the use of deliberative procedures without endorsing the three basic ideas?

He argues that these questions can be answered in the affirmative for those engaged in deliberative practical rationality. This is based on what he calls two facts:

1   When we engage in public deliberation we do indeed endorse the 'Project of Justice' (we agree that we should try, to the extent that we can, to construct a society in which all include each other and themselves, in solidarity, as free and equal).
2   When we engage in public deliberation we do indeed accept the 'Fact of Widespread Moral Disagreement' (we recognise that we do not immediately agree on our interpretations of what the basic ideas of solidarity, equality and freedom demand from us in different contexts of social life).

These facts, however, do not constitute rational grounds but are intuitive or intentional grounds for public deliberation.They are in other words explicit moral positions. The essence of Gilabert's (2005a: 199) expressive elaboration proposal lies in the fact that 'not all, but only first-level substantive claims need to be shown to pass the test of public deliberation'. He defends the rational–deliberative grounds of his proposal as follows:

> Public deliberation provides a way to elaborate our ideas of solidarity, freedom, and equality in the face of disagreement while expressing them in the very activity of their elaboration. This is what makes the deliberative procedure morally important. It is flexible because it does not presuppose the prioritisation of any ethical conception of the good life or any specific, first order moral rules and provides, rather, a 'formula' for assessing them. But it is not empty either, because the project of justice . . . animates its emergence and use. Via public deliberation we search for answers to the questions 'what solidarity?', 'freedom from what and to what?', and 'equality of what?' while expressing rather than giving up our solidaristic, egalitarian, and libertarian motivations in the very practice of making sense of them.
>
> (Gilabert, 2005b: 199)

The question now is how we can determine what the three levels of substance mean for the facilitation of research in transformative partnerships; partnerships in which we will disagree systematically on what our basic ideas specifically mean for practice. This question is addressed in the next section.

Facilitation of research in transformative research partnerships as hospitality

Transformative partnerships and their facilitation – in our interpretation – are based on Gilabert's second order norms: norms that are derived from general ideals (third order norms) and which determine the practices of decision-making and justification concerning the first order norms. In the introduction to this book we define transformative facilitation of practitioner research as a reciprocal relationship. Reciprocal, according to Maiter, Simich, Jacobson and Wise (2008: 305), is 'an ongoing process of exchange with the aim of establishing and maintaining equality between parties'. This view contrasts with the transactional model, in which facilitation is seen as the provision of resources and skills to be handed on from one party to another. The shift from the transactional to the transformative model of facilitation is often explained on pragmatic–empirical grounds: research has shown that teachers rarely use the resources and skills transferred to them in academic courses in their work as practising teachers. A transformative model seems to be more effective. The shift from the one model to the other reflects, however, also changes in normative views about authority and these changes have a substantive but not empirical basis.

The transactional model reflects a hierarchical view of authority: the educator or facilitator decides what will be transferred, how that will be done and how it is to be assessed. It is a linear research, development and dissemination model: the researcher has the expertise and authority to research; the educator or facilitator has the authority to transfer general academic knowledge and the teacher has a duty to apply what he or she has learnt. According to Van Stokkum (2011), such authority is rejected in many democratic social theories, because it is equated with paternalism and curtailment of independent judgement. In its place comes the idea that freedom is the same as 'persuasion with argument', that is freedom through dialogue. The dialogue itself must also be free from dominance by experts. However, Van Stokkum (2011) argued that in Western societies this ideal of freedom has gradually led to what he calls 'emotional democracy', a democracy in which autonomy has become the dictatorship of individual self-development accompanied by the withholding of criticism. Tackling people about their choices and behaviour is seen as 'interference' and annoying rather than an opening up of dialogue, which actually is the aim of transformative partnerships, as is argued in Chapter 6 on communicability. When dialogue is annoyed autonomy it becomes 'an invitation to close yourself off from discussion about what might be harmful or indecent behaviour and an order to others to let it pass' (Van Stokkum, 2011: 29, translation by the author).

This emotional democracy can lead to relativism and subjectivism. For example, reflection in professional development often never gets beyond 'What did I do?, What did I feel about it? and What do I do next?' Then all that remains is the argument: 'That's the way I felt about it and there's an end to the matter'. Faced with this kind of emotional view of authority, educators have no option other than to rely on procedures, rules, standards and competitive lists. This backs up Furedi (2009) who argued that many people have started to see authority as the opposite of freedom and that is precisely what is putting our freedom in jeopardy. This is why Van Stokkum (2011) argued for a relational way of looking at autonomy and revitalisation of informal authority. He based his argument on Hannah Arendt's (1954) modernising interpretation, which is that authority can have a creative capacity. Taking personal responsibility is central to this and this responsibility is risky because the outcome is unpredictable. This is in line with the reference in Chapter 3 to Stenhouse's notion of emancipation as the 'intellectual, moral and spiritual autonomy which we recognise when we eschew paternalism and the rule of authority and hold ourselves obliged to appeal to judgement' (1979: 163).

Van Stokkum (2011) then goes on to argue that developing autonomy is dependent on contextual factors such as 'the availability of support and being allowed to learn through trial and error'. These factors should be seen as the essence of research in transformative partnerships. After all, we do not automatically make the right choices, Van Stokkum (2011) argues:

> We can make mistakes and through fear, ignorance or a penchant for conventions we can close ourselves off to alternative choices. Because of this we need guidance from empathetic people who can bring alternative perspectives to our attention. This enables us to put our own wishes into perspective or to reposition them, to learn to nuance our own views and not take them too seriously. To make progress and to broaden our horizons, therefore, we need targets outside ourselves: we need people who can support us and make us stronger.
>
> (p. 29, translation by the author)

In line with Van Stokkum's (2011) social theory, this support in transformative partnerships can be defined as hospitality, which in essence is about 'sharing a finite space'. As a participant in that space you are a temporary guest and you share that space with others. The academic facilitator as host can take the lead in that space and is responsible for ensuring that the situation in hand proceeds to a good outcome. He or she introduces asymmetry into the relationships, not to emphasise or perpetuate hierarchical relationships, but to make things go smoothly and take responsibility for proper regulation of public deliberation and rational argument about 'what is' and 'what ought to be'. This authority may be temporary and other participants may take over the role of host. In Chapter 4 for instance a case is presented in which local authorities and teachers took over the role of the academic facilitators in order to create sustainable partnerships in the local community. In ARTE (Ponte 2002a and b), it was also found that taking over authority in partnerships really does happen given time. I, as the academic facilitator, first acted as a host for the teacher educators and the teachers. I initiated and designed the general framework of the project in which facilitators and their teachers should be enabled to start and to continue. As the project progressed, teacher educators and teachers (in that order) increasingly took the lead themselves. An illustration of how this process developed is presented in the next section.

The process towards facilitation as hospitality

The ARTE study (Ponte, 2002a and b; Ponte, Ax, Beijaard and Verloop, 2004) concluded in the first place that the teachers, and to a lesser extent the teacher educators, needed a reasonable period of unbroken time to master the substantive principles of action research in partnerships. This seemed to be inherent in the fact that it was through experience that they learned to put flesh on these principles, by increasingly interpreting those experiences collaboratively and by making sense of them in terms of both substance and the procedures of research partnerships. Developing a common language seems to be important therefore. Furthermore it turned out that participants had to get used to the non-voluntary nature of action research, that is to say that they increasingly had to reveal what they were doing and especially why they were doing it. Teachers often found this threatening at first and it was accompanied by feelings of insecurity. Because of this many teachers would not do their action research without the support of others and some even developed an aversion to action research (despite the fact that their participation in ARTE was voluntary). That goes part of the way to explaining why action research was sometimes difficult to keep going. Based on these experiences, it was hypothesised that even teachers who already had experience with action research would need to be challenged and supported by others. The teachers in ARTE turned out to accept support more easily and use it more effectively as they developed a number of professional orientations. These orientations will be illustrated using the experiences of Tom (one of the ARTE teachers).

- *Orientation to practice*: Practice conceived as one's own action at a given moment from which something can be learned with a view to one's own action in the future.

At first Tom wanted to set up a pupil monitoring system that would then have to be implemented by his colleagues throughout the school. He wanted to evaluate whether that happened only after the implementation. He thought that he would research others' actions as an 'external researcher'. He said to his facilitator:

> You are always talking about 'your' own practice, it is always 'I': 'how I know', 'how I involve' and so on. But the problem is that my practice isn't there yet. The teacher in the example you gave us had her own practice and she could change it, she had her own way of teaching and her own relationship with the pupils. But when I want to talk about introducing a pupil monitoring system, we haven't got one yet. I am starting from scratch and so it is difficult for me to research that. I don't have a practice yet.

The facilitator explained that activities undertaken with others to introduce a pupil monitoring system is also practice (current practice) and that Tom could, for instance, focus on what his role is in this process (joint practice).

- *Orientation to research*: Research conceived as the repeated systematic gathering and interpretation of data about one's own action with a view to trying out improvements step by step and continuously evaluating the desired and actual impacts.

Tom initially had the idea that doing research meant administering one-off, large-scale surveys with questionnaires and that he as the researcher 'must be objective', in particular by not researching his own practice but specifically by researching the practice of others. Later he said about his own action research:

> This method of examining yourself and your work is new to me. It is not so difficult; we could do it more often. And what I've learned from this is that if you want to change something, you have to do it yourself and that you then have to systematically map out what is going on and why.

- *Orientation to understanding*: Understanding conceived as 'knowing the what, how and why' of their practices; knowing as something that can be gradually developed through critical analysis and conceptualisation; knowing that can be adapted by reading, doing and in dialogue with others.

Tom explained:

> I expected action research to be a very clear and simple way of working. Rather like that technique for meetings that we learned on the communication course during our study. You simply say: that is a technique that everyone can understand and that is quick to use. So folks, let's just solve this problem. Now I can see that it doesn't work like that: step-by-step is often better than going too fast. Knowledge does not exist, knowledge grows!

- *Orientation to initiative*: Role conceived as taking responsibility oneself for the content and progress of one's action research.

Tom wrote in the beginning:

> In the next few weeks I'm going to do the homework set by the facilitator, so that I'm able to put my questions into words when we get to that stage.

Later he wrote:

> I have formulated my research question by myself and have now planned my explorative phase. I have a number of questions about them. I decided to discuss these questions in the facilitation meeting.

- *Orientation to demarcation*: Action research conceived as taking aspects of practice as projects to work on with a longer-term perspective.

Tom was used to 'working on everything at the same time in an ad hoc way' and also to exchanging experiences with his colleagues informally as and when he wanted to. At first he expected to do the same thing in the ARTE programme. He asked himself:

> What is so special about action research? This kind of discussion with colleagues is part of the way I normally work.

However, the facilitator explained to him that:

> In action research you tell yourself: we want to work on this aspect over a rather longer period and we hope that by doing this we will achieve this and that; the rest of our practice simply continues as normal and for the time being we let ourselves be satisfied with that.

As Tom himself put it later on:

> With action research it is about working on one issue at a time and about doing that thoughtfully. It is about the small steps. Not starting with how you think you are doing, but carefully examining how you are really doing and if that is what you really want to do. It is a gradual process; don't make such a drama of it if it goes a bit less quickly than your other work.

- *Orientation to functionality*: Action research conceived as a whole range of activities, in which one activity is deliberately used to review an earlier activity and/or plan the next activity.

Tom's group began their action research with a card game that was intended to help them to define their moral position. Next they were asked to keep a diary on the further progress of their action research. In response to the facilitator's question about how the reflections in his diary compared with the results from the card game, Tom replied:

> There was no connection at all between the card game and the diary! When I started to keep the diary, I did it because the facilitator said I had to. It was nothing more than an interesting method of self-examination. I found the card game fascinating but didn't attach any importance to it. Only weeks

later did I see in my diary that I had a moral problem in my lower school classes and that I would have to work on that first.

As the ARTE project went on, the teacher educators progressed from a linear, transactional form of guidance (that is getting the teachers to carry out the separate action research steps in sequence) to recurrent facilitation on-the-job. The more they followed up on what was happening on the ground, the more successful their facilitation turned out to be. This meant that the teacher educators had to get used to the fact that the meetings with the teachers could not be planned in detail beforehand: 'It is weird going to the schools without a fixed programme and pre-selected literature that we as facilitators give the teachers to read.' They also had to get used to the fact that what the teachers contributed to the meetings could be interpreted together on the spot.

At first the teacher educators saw this – for them new – approach to facilitation as an identical role to the 'critical friend' role among the teachers themselves, a role that they perceived as mainly responsive: 'Teachers have to be responsible for their own action research and so they have to try to discover the methods and principles for themselves.' However, this passive approach to facilitation was found to be inadequate, because teachers needed concrete guidelines in order to be able to do their action research and because they had to be challenged to do things that they were not used to doing and which they would not have got around to on their own. During the course of the project the facilitators – through dialogue with the academic researcher and the teachers – developed a more successful inductive approach to facilitation. I was able to identify five characteristics of this, which will be illustrated here using the quotes from Jane (facilitator) and Eli (teacher).

- *Cyclic*, by continually getting teachers to look back (What have I done and why?) and forward (How can I progress from here and why?).

A teacher, Eli, was confused about what her next step would be in terms of research. Her facilitator, Jane, wrote in her logbook:

> At this meeting I explained the steps of action research to Eli again. Although I had done it before, I tried to make links again with her, both back to the research question and her explorations so far, and forward to the action for improvement.

- *Explicit*, by making explicit what teachers are doing and expressing it in terms of action research methodology.

At the meeting Jane looked at the plan of activities Eli was working on for her action research. Then after the meeting Eli wrote:

> I said that I had hardly been able to do anything at all. But when the facilitator questioned me it turned out that I had already done some things with regard to changing my pupil guidance role. I realised that I was already working on my actions for improvement. By asking questions the facilitator made me realise that this was also part of my action research.

- *Negotiated*, by exploring with the teachers by force of argument the best way to act in the given circumstances.

After the first cycle of her research Eli wanted to develop policy at departmental level by writing a policy document and giving this to her colleagues. However, Jane, as her facilitator, thought that she should also link school policy to her own scope for action and her research. She asked Eli what she thought about this. The following conversation took place between them on this issue:

Eli: I think we need to sit down with teachers and put down a clear vision about what we expect in the area of co-operation.

Jane: What would your contribution to this be?

Eli: I can galvanise it. First I will talk to my colleagues.

Jane: Would it also be possible to try something out yourself and get the discussion going at the same time?

Eli: Yes, but I would like the school to get more benefit from ARTE.

Jane: What needs to change in your opinion, if the school is to get more benefit from it?

Eli: I think we need to agree to give ARTE more priority.

Jane: Yes, and if you look at the content, are there requirements you would like to lay down there? You are all looking at individual questions. Do you want to make that more general?

Eli: Next year I would like to work collaboratively on the same theme with the group. Of course, it would be nice, for instance, to have a clearer idea myself about 'co-operative learning', but next year I lose my group of pupils and it wouldn't be finished.

Jane: So you want the group to focus on one theme?

Eli: Not only that, also on one target group, the Social Care Department for instance.

In the end they agreed on this plan: the group would work collaboratively on policy development by choosing a common theme, namely independent work in the Social Care Department. Within this theme, teachers would work on their own issues individually or in pairs.

- *Forceful*, by giving teachers more and more responsibility for actually doing what they planned to do and also for really discussing this with the other participants in a systematic and purposeful way.

Before one of the meetings in the second ARTE year, Jane wrote:

> Last year I was too much of a follower. I want to speed things up now. Last year everyone got stuck in the explorative phase of their action research. I want to get the progress of the action research planned at the meeting and to get everyone to write up his or her plans into concrete activities.

After the meeting:

> We went through the situation item by item with all the members of the group. I urged them to get down to concrete activities. We started with Eli's planning. We looked at how much time each step would need and what could possibly be left out. Clear agreements were reached. Everyone has an idea of what he or she will be doing over the coming period.

- *Critical*, by continually asking teachers what they are doing and why that particular thing.

Jane reported, for instance:

> Teachers often have the idea that if only you did things differently it would be better. I have started to use the guiding questions, for instance, to question why they think it is an improvement, for whom and what assumptions they are making. This morning Eli told us that the pupils had become quieter as a result of her actions for improvement. Then I asked: quieter, yes and . . . why is that better? Is that what you hoped to achieve? And 'evidence' often crops up. This morning, for example, the teachers in the group spontaneously started to ask each other: You have made a number of assumptions, but how do you know they are true?

Final remarks: interplay between the scope for professional decision-making and the scope for professional action

In the previous section of this chapter, the experiences of the educators and teachers were used to illustrate how they left behind traditional and instrumental ideas about research and increasingly directed their efforts at research, which gives a more central place to defining problems and justifying substantive claims together. One of the ways this was expressed was in the fact that the partners in the project increasingly built reciprocal links between what, in Chapter 1, we called *substantive and functional rationality*. We have also demonstrated in this chapter that the building of these reciprocal links in their decision-making went hand-in-hand with the development of facilitation into a form of 'hospitality' (Van Stokkum, 2011), a form of guidance in which the leading and facilitative role of the academic researcher is seen as temporary and one which is gradually shared with both the facilitators and the teachers. The change of roles will be further explored in relation to sustainability (Chapter 4), professional learning (Chapter 5) and communicability (Chapter 6).

The question that can be asked now is what conditions enabled the developments to take place. In the introduction we did after all claim that we wanted to look at the facilitation of research in transformative partnerships not only from the perspective of 'professionals as human beings who are capable of acting autonomously and rationally' but also from 'the cultural, social and political contexts in which they act'. In the context described in Chapter 1, we linked this question with Habermas's theory (1981) on *lifeworld* and *system*, assuming that the scope for professional action is determined by the interplay between *system* and *lifeworld*. This will be examined in more detail in Chapter 3 using the idea of nested contexts at global, national and local levels. However, it is clear that a number of issues with regard to contexts that emerged in ARTE deserve further attention (Ponte 2002a and b; Ponte, Ax, Beijaard and Verloop, 2004).

The process in transformative research partnerships and its facilitation does not always seem to be straightforward when the people involved have no experience of it, as in ARTE. It was a process of trial and error together. Both facilitators and teachers had a tendency to ascribe the sometimes laborious course of action research to clearly identifiable system factors such as lack of time, timetabling problems and organisational problems caused by, for instance, reorganisations and mergers.

A teacher wrote:

> We find ourselves in a chaotic situation because of the merger. Three cultures have been merged. The resources were too late. There are a lot of

timetabling problems and the management are not all on the same wavelength. Many management problems are being put on the plates of teachers under the guise of 'self-directing teams'. There is a lot of grumbling and complaining. The result of all this is that more and more teachers fail to do what has been agreed and are going their own way. Ceasing to feel responsible for the organisation is becoming a trend. Many teachers are going off sick. I myself am pessimistic about the current developments but I do my utmost to remain inspired. I've lost half of my lessons and I'm the only English teacher in the team who is still working.

System factors like this certainly restricted the scope for professional decision-making and action (*lifeworld*) and therefore impeded the progress of research in transformative partnerships. Nevertheless we learned that the relationship between *system* and *lifeworld* was more complicated than this suggests. The difficulties that teachers and facilitators had when they first attempted to conduct or facilitate research in transformative partnerships can, we believe, be better understood as the difficulty that they themselves had in moving from a one-sided *functional rationality* to a more *substantive rationality*. They needed as it were to shake off their instrumental thinking and actions, at a time when those kinds of ideas and actions are dominant in all parts of modern society, including in the institutions where the participants in the partnerships are working. As was stated in the beginning of this chapter, making such change requires professionals to have the courage to think and act beyond the well-trodden paths.

We could also say that their own instrumental thinking and actions within the confines of the well-trodden paths do, as Kemmis and Grootenboer (2008) say, function as mediating preconditions for subsequent practices. A number of teachers were uncertain about formulating the aim and content of their research themselves, because they felt a strong moral pressure to 'do something that will benefit the school immediately'. This often involved implementing changes imposed by policy, as they realised that 'doing something conceived by others is safer and less confrontational'. The purposeful communication with colleagues about the what, how and why of their research was also new for ARTE participants. For instance, they had to get used to the fact that this was no longer a voluntary activity. A teacher said:

In a hectic day at school it is often difficult to find time to meet as a group. At the end of the first project year we were thinking about stopping. In the end we decided to carry on after all and to face up to the consequences of this decision. At the last meeting we told the facilitator that we had decided to give real priority to ARTE. So that means that we have to meet regularly and stick to our agreements. I will put the meeting dates in my diary.

Another teacher said:

> The valuable thing about action research is that you are very conscious of practising your profession. But the difficult thing is that you cannot just get on and do something. You have to take all kinds of steps that you would not take otherwise. You have to force yourself to do that, because it is often about rather long-term goals. I'm always inclined to give priority to ad hoc things.

Her facilitator commented:

> I've noticed that the teachers in my group prefer it when I exercise soft pressure to get them to keep to their agreements. But in my experience up to now this often stops at the planning and the plans are hardly ever brought to fruition.

In transformative partnerships, partners are therefore challenged to step out in a new direction. That always involves uncertainty, but if it works builds confidence and gives people a huge sense of empowerment and capability. A few of the many positive experiences reported by ARTE participants are reproduced below.
Facilitators:

> We found that you not only influence your own action but also the situation in which you are practising. We now have a better idea of what we want to achieve.

Teachers:

> We found that if you want something you can do together, that you don't have to always do everything on your own, that you don't have to have everything under control beforehand. We are also dealing with the context in which we work differently. We've brought more openness into school and we engage in dialogue with colleagues and school management more frequently. Surprisingly enough that has been very much appreciated. Facilitators often ask about things such as: Have you also asked the pupils about that? How do you know that your assumptions are right? For whom is that change an improvement? What are your aims and how far have you got with them?

Their thinking and actions then function in a way as mediating conditions for adopting explicit moral positions and trying to realise 'what is desirable but not yet existing'. That is always a position of hope and uncertainty at the same time, according to Neiman (2008: 141): 'The gap between what is and what should be is too deep to ever be reached completely, but what we can hope to do is to fill it in.'

This hope was the underlying motive for ARTE and based on experiences with this project we are able to conclude that facilitation of research in transformative partnerships should not be only directed at conducting the research as such. It is about more than that. It is about developing a substantive stance, geared to both the active adoption and justification of moral choices and the active enlargement of the scope for professional decision-making and action in order to be able to give these choices concrete substance.

References

Arendt, H. (1954). *The human condition. Between past and future.* Harmondsworth: Penguin.

Atkinson, E. (2000). In defence of ideas, or why 'what works' is not enough. *British Journal of Sociology of Education, 21*(3): 307–330.

Ax, J. and Ponte, P. (2010). Moral issues in educational praxis: A perspective from pedagogiek and didactiek as human sciences in continental Europe. *Pedagogy, Culture & Society, 18*(1): 29–42.

Barone, D.F., Maddux, J.E. and Snyder, C.R. (1997). *Social cognitive psychology. History and current times.* New York: Plenum Press.

Biesta, G.J.J. (2007). Why 'what works' won't work: Evidence-based practice and the democratic deficit in educational research. *Educational Theory, 57*(1): 1–22.

Biesta, G.J.J. (2010a). *Good education in an age of measurement: Ethics, politics, democracy.* Boulder: Paradigm Publishers.

Biesta, G.J.J. (2010b). Why 'what works' still won't work. From evidence-based education to value-based education. *Studies in Philosophy and Education 29*(5): 491–503.

Blackmore, J. (2002). Is it only 'what works' that counts in new knowledge economies? Evidence-based practice, educational research and teacher education in Australia. *Social Policy and Society, 1*(3): 257–266.

Carr, W. and Kemmis, S. (1986). *Becoming critical.* London: The Falmer Press.

Dewey, J. (1929/1930). The sources of a science of education. In J.A. Boydston (Ed.) *The later works: vol. 5, 1929–1930* (pp. 3–40). Carbondale: Southern Illinois University Press.

Dilthey, W. (1914). *Einleitung in die Geisteswissenschaften. Versuch einer Grundlegung für das Studium der Gesellschaft und der Geschichte.* [Introduction to the human sciences. Attempt to lay a foundation for the study of society and of history.] Göttingen: Vandenhoeck & Ruprecht.

Elliott, J. (1991). *Action research for educational change.* Buckingham: Open University Press.

Furedi, F. (2009). *Why education is not educating.* London: Continuum Press.

Gilabert, P. (2005a). A substantivist construal of discourse ethics. *International Journal of Philosophical Studies, 13*(3): 405–437.

Gilabert, P. (2005b). The substantive dimension of deliberative practical rationality. *Philosophy Social Critisisme, 31*(2): 185–210.

Gilabert, P. (2006). Considerations on the notion of moral validity in the moral theories of Kant and Habermas. *Kant Studien, 97*, 211–227.

Habermas, J. (1981). *Theorie des kommunikativen Handelns.* [Theory of communicative action.] Frankfurt: Suhrkamp.

Kant, E. (Eds A.W. Wood and P. Guyer) (1999). *The Cambridge edition of the works of Immanuel Kant: Critique of pure reason.* Cambridge: Cambridge University Press.

Karstanje, P. (2007). Professionalism and leadership in Dutch education. In J. Ax and P. Ponte (Eds), *Critiquing praxis. Conceptual and empirical trends in the teaching profession* (pp. 113–126). Rotterdam: Sense Publishers.

Kemmis, S. (2001). Exploring the relevance of critical theory for action research: Emancipatory action research in the footsteps of Jürgen Habermas. In P. Reason and H. Bradbury (Eds), *Handbook of action research* (pp. 91–102). London: Sage Publishers.

Kemmis, S. and Grootenboer, P. (2008) Situating praxis in practice: Practice architectures and the cultural, social and material conditions for practice. In S. Kemmis and T. Smith (Eds) *Enabling praxis: Challenges for education.* Rotterdam: Sense.

Lewin, K. (1947). Frontiers in group dynamics II: Channels of group life; social planning and action research. *Human Relations, 1*: 143–153.

Maiter, S., Simich, L., Jacobson, N. and Wise, J. (2008). Reciprocity: An ethic for participatory action research with culturally diverse communities. *Action Research, 6*(3): 305–325.

Mertens, D.M. (2009). *Transformative research and evaluation.* New York: London.

Neiman, S. (2008). *Moral clarity: a guide for grown-up idealists* (1st edition). Orlando: Harcourt.

Ponte, P. (2002a). How teachers become action researchers and how teacher educators become their facilitators. *Educational Action Research Journal, 10*(3): 399–423.

Ponte, P. (2002b). *Actieonderzoek door docenten: Uitvoering en begeleiding in theorie en praktijk.* [Action research by teachers: Performance and facilitation in theory and practice.] PhD thesis. Apeldoorn/Leuven: Garant.

Ponte, P. (2009). *Gedrag en onderzoek in de educatieve praxis: Plaatsbepaling.* [Behaviour and research in educational praxis: An orientation.] Inaugural speech (Dutch and English version: www.educatie.onderzoek.hu.nl/Data/Press/gedrag-en-onderzoek-in-de-educatieve-praxis, accessed 1 June 2012). Utrecht: Hogeschool Utrecht.

Ponte, P. (2010). Met karikaturen zijn geen werelden te winnen. [Worlds cannot be won with caricatures.] *Tijdschrift voor Orthopedagogiek, 49*(6): 269–276.

Ponte, P. and Ax, J. (2011). Action research in teacher education: A matter of praxis? In N. Mockler and J. Sachs (Eds) *Completing the circle: Practitioner research with and for teachers and students.* London: Springer Publishers.

Ponte, P. and Rönnerman, K. (2009). Reflections on trends in action research. *Educational Action Research Journal, 17*(1): 115–169.

Ponte, P., Ax, J., Beijaard, D. and Verloop, T. (2004). Teachers' development of professional knowledge through action research and the facilitation of this by teacher educators. *Teaching and Teacher Education, 20*: 517–588.

Riedel, H. (1977). *Allgemeine Didaktik und unterrichtliche Praxis: Eine Einführung*
[Moral issues in educational praxis: A perspective.] München: Kösel-Verlag.

Stenhouse, L. (1975). *An introduction to curriculum research and development*. London:
Heinemann Educational Books.

Stenhouse, L. (1979). The problems of standards in illuminative research. *Scottish
Educational Review, 11*(1): 5–10.

Van Stokkum, B. (2011). Revitalisering van informeel gezag: Gezag en vrijheid verzoend.
[Revitalising informal authority: authority and freedom reconciled.] *Algemeen
Nederlands Tijdschrift voor Wijsbegeerte, 1*(103): 21–35.

Zeichner, K. and Liston, D. (1986). An inquiry-oriented approach to student teaching.
Journal of Teaching Practice [Australian], *6*(1): 5–24.

Chapter 3

Politics

The lead author of this chapter is Nicole Mockler, who has facilitated practitioner research and other forms of inquiry-based professional learning in a broad range of Australian schools and project contexts. Much of Nicole's research focuses on the links between education policy and practice, and the politics of education, and this chapter aims to examine these in reference to the possibility of 'transformational partnerships' offered by facilitated practitioner research.

As Carr and Kemmis (2010) have strenuously argued, critical educational action research is, much like education itself, always an intensely political enterprise. As we argued in Chapter 1, the act of facilitation of practitioner inquiry is shaped in the interplay between *lifeworld* and *system* and *substantive* and *functional rationality*, such that the aim is to broaden the scope of both action and decision-making in the context within which it is enacted. This chapter will examine the politics of facilitated practitioner inquiry from three standpoints, which we see as 'nested' political contexts. We argue that these three political contexts, namely the global education policy context, the context of the national and the local micro-political context of the school and research team, each have their own impact upon the shape of the work that is possible and also upon the role of the facilitator. Indeed, these three contexts also impact upon the capacity of practitioner research to be transformative and by that substantive, as discussed in Chapter 2. Furthermore, we see that a key dimension to the effective facilitation of practitioner inquiry is the mediation of these political contexts (to varying extents), and for this reason we have dedicated this chapter to the discussion of politics and their impact. Facilitation of practitioner inquiry, we believe, should be a transformative rather than merely transactional practice, and an understanding of the political contexts within which the work is located is essential to this transformative dimension.

The notion of 'practice architectures', discussed at some length in Chapter 1, is a useful lens through which to view these political contexts and their interplay with facilitated practitioner research. In a recent article, Stephen Kemmis (2009) outlines the 'densely interwoven patterns of saying, doing and relating that enable and constrain each new interaction' (p. 466), constituting architectures of practice. He names the following as practice architectures that provide mediating preconditions for practice, shaping and forming the *praxis* of the individuals who operate within them:

(1) *cultural–discursive* preconditions, which shape and give content to the 'thinking' and 'saying' that orient and justify practices;

(2) *material–economic* preconditions, which shape and give content to the 'doing' of the practice; and

(3) *social–political preconditions*, which shape and give content to the 'relatings' involved in the practice.

(Kemmis, 2009: 466)

We contend that each of the three political contexts named above intersect with and impact upon these practice architectures such that particular 'sayings, doings and relatings' are in part produced by the political context itself, enacted, of course, in varying ways in different educational contexts. While it could be claimed that each of the political contexts aligns most readily with one or other of the sets of preconditions named above, we see the intersections and manifestations as a complex web wherein all three contexts link in different forms to each of the sets of preconditions, and will take this up in the discussion below.

This chapter is divided into three parts, with one focused on each of the above-named political contexts and the dilemmas it entails for practitioner researchers and those who support and facilitate their work.

Global education policy contexts

While 'educational borrowing and lending' (Steiner-Khamsi, 2004) on a global scale has long been a feature of education policy in Western countries, as Rizvi and Lingard have argued (2010), the context of globalisation over the past two decades has seen an unprecedented rise in the possibilities regarding global education policy. As the 'neoliberal social imaginary' (Rizvi and Lingard, 2010: 8, ff.) has taken hold of Western democracies, a number of educational 'themes' have emerged and been played out to varying degrees in many Western countries, such that neo-liberal thinking has permeated education policy on a series of fronts, globally.

In his 2001 book, Michael Apple pointed to the rise of neo-liberalism in education, aligning neo-liberal ideology with a kind of 'market fundamentalism' (Apple, 2001, 2006) that privileges first and foremost the common sense of the market and therefore what can be crudely measured and quantified over those elements that are more complex and ephemeral. While Rizvi and Lingard, in their recent book,

express some hope that the tight reign of neo-liberal ideologies might have been broken by their demonstrated failure displayed on an international scale in the global financial crisis of 2008, three years after its eruption we can see no observable retreat from neo-liberal education policy and indeed perhaps in some ways an even tighter clinging to the power of 'the market' can be detected in some countries. The 'Race to the Top' programme, introduced by the Obama administration three months after the emergence of the global financial crisis and recent policy discussion in Australia of the introduction of performance pay for teachers based on standardised testing results are two examples of the continuing manifestation of neo-liberal ideologies in education beyond the global financial crisis.

The increased linking of education to economic outcomes, known in Australia as 'the productivity agenda', wherein education is seen not as a process of developing an informed and critically aware citizenry but rather is primarily valued for the contribution educated citizens might make to the country's *economy*, has worked to gradually separate educational discourse from the realm of democracy and participation and implanted it instead in the realm of economics and 'workforce participation'. In Bourdieuian terms, this has seen the dominant 'logic of practice' of the all-powerful field of economics, which has become increasingly responsible for framing the constitution of 'society' in the eyes of governments over the past two decades, encroach increasingly on the field of education to the point where issues of measurement, quantification and instrumentalism (*functional rationality*) have taken on a privileged role, at the expense of a more nuanced substantive appreciation of the field.

This neo-liberal social imaginary has manifested globally in education in many ways. We elaborate on three key themes: standards and accountability, teacher quality and parental choice. These three overlapping themes, each with implications for the quantification and measurement of various dimensions of education, have pervaded education policy across much of the Western world over the past decade and at the time of writing show no signs of abating, despite critique and criticism from many educators from both progressive and conservative backgrounds (see for example Ravitch, 2010). While none of these three policy agendas is strictly about classroom practice, each of them provides an important part of the context of teachers' work in the current age, and holds significant implications for the enactment of inquiry-based professional learning and facilitated practitioner research. They work to influence and frame the cultural–discursive, material–economic and social–political preconditions of educational practice through the ways in which they shape educational discourse in the public domain. Furthermore, this need not be a one-way relationship: the kind of activist professionalism (Sachs, 2003) embodied in transformational partnerships provides opportunities for the scope of rational decision-making and autonomous action discussed in Chapter 1 to be enlarged. The key here lies in understanding the agendas and the links between them.

The standards and accountability agenda

The discourse of standards and accountability in education is multifaceted and, as Peter Taubman argues, has moved at a rapid pace to shape education in the twenty-first century. He argues succinctly that its constituent parts are

> tests, which are the lynchpin of the transformation; the language of public policy, which drives the transformation; the discourses and assemblages of business practices associated with neoliberal economic policies and what British anthropologists call audit culture, discourses and practices that have accelerated the standardization and quantification of educational experience and turned it into an education market worth billions of dollars; the rhetoric of blame and fear and the promulgation of heroic narratives of exemplary teachers, which, coupled with the wide-spread use of tests, render teachers and teacher educators susceptible to the language of policy and the lure of business practices and make possible teachers' psychic investment in various aspects of the transformation; and, finally, the ascendancy of the learning sciences, which have annexed pedagogy and curriculum to applied psychology and provided the points of translation or the bridges between educational discourses and the discursive and non-discursive practices of the business world.
>
> (Taubman, 2009: 12–13)

For Taubman, the centrepiece of the standards and accountability agenda is standardised testing, which has reflexively impacted those other constituent parts, and it is this facet of standards and accountability that we shall focus on in this discussion.

Embedded strongly in the US in the *No Child Left Behind* reforms of the George W. Bush era, standardised testing has emerged as one of the key education policy trajectories on a global scale. Described by Gordon Stobart in his book *Testing Times: The Uses and Abuses of Assessment* (2008) as 'the pull of standardisation', exemplified where 'a concern for a particular interpretation of reliability (same task, same test conditions, external marking or marking scheme), narrows the range of what can be initiated by the school or the individual student'. He continues on to argue:

> The pull [of standardisation] is particularly strong when the results are used for accountability purposes . . . If the results of schools are going to be compared, then, the argument goes, the schools ought to be doing the same tests and tasks. It is this same-for-all concern which has often dogged moves to more systematically valid assessment.
>
> (Stobart, 2008: 104–105)

In the context of the neo-liberal social imaginary, standardised testing is thus conceptualised as 'objective' assessment, positioned in a bipolar dichotomy against assessment that relies on the flaws of bias enacted in teacher professional judgement, and thus capable of holding teachers (and therefore, schools) to account for the quality of learning undertaken by their students.

The teacher quality agenda

As Taubman points out in the quotation above, the teacher quality agenda is linked to standardised testing and the rise of standards and accountability in education through the notion, embedded in neo-liberal educational discourses, that teachers are responsible for the failure of students and schools to meet testing targets. These ideas, of course, run contrary to more expansive and holistic views of teachers and their work (Biesta, 2007; Ponte and Ax, 2011).

In most Western countries, teacher standards are positioned as an attempt to raise the quality of the teaching profession. In countries such as England, the United States, Australia and the Netherlands, these standards have formed the basis for accreditation processes with the dual purposes of providing a level of 'quality assurance' (to borrow from the discourse of business and economics) and positioning teaching in some way alongside those 'real' professions such as medicine and law. The tangible connection of teacher quality to standardised testing through the introduction of performance pay based on test results has further cemented this relationship, bringing teachers and governments into a dangerous deal that risks sacrificing good student learning to expediently improved test scores.

Within the teacher quality agenda, we have seen a shift in the past decade in many Western countries from a discourse focused on teaching quality to one focused on teacher quality (Mockler, 2011a). The shift is a subtle but important one. Embedded in a focus on teaching quality is a desire to support and foster teacher professional learning, to encourage pedagogical and curricular innovation and risk taking and to collaboratively determine and pursue good teaching practice. Conversely, embedded in the ensuing focus on teacher quality is a desire to narrowly measure and quantify teachers' work (represented simply in test scores), to standardise practice and attribute blame to teachers where their students fail to measure up. The significance of sound and effective professional learning is largely absent from this discourse, despite reminders issued to governments that countries such as Finland, where results on standardised international tests are seen as enviable, have generally low levels of surveillance of teachers and high budgets earmarked for teacher professional learning, having purposefully rejected the impetus of what Sahlberg in his work on educational reform in Finland terms the 'global educational reform movement' (2004, 2007, 2009). As Linda Darling-Hammond (2011) reminds us, 'you can't fire your way to Finland':

punitive measures against teachers for perceived ineffectiveness and poor practice are unlikely to be as successful as generative professional learning in creating a strong and effective teaching profession.

Teacher standards and accreditation have not been the only policy solution implemented in attempts to solve the 'problem' of teacher quality. An associated policy solution is the by-passing of traditional teacher education and teacher educators through fast tracking schemes such as *Teach for America*, which was founded in 1990 and its more recently established international counterparts such as *Teach First*, founded in the UK in 2002 and now the largest provider of pre-service teacher education in the country, *Teach for Australia* and *Teach First Deutschland*, both established in 2009. In 2007, Wendy Kopp, the founder of *Teach for America* established *Teach for All*, an organisation focused on replicating the *Teach for America* model worldwide. *Teach for China, Teach for India, Teach First Israel, Empieza por Educar* in Ecquador, *Iespējamā Misija (Mission Possible)* in Latvia and *Noored Kooli (Youth to School)* in Estonia are all recently established programmes under the auspices of *Teach for All*. Clearly these alternate entry pathways purportedly designed to eradicate inequality in education are now global in scale and pervasive in their reach as teacher education programmes, underpinned by an assumption that teaching comprises a series of functional-rational skills that can be taught in a short space of time and practiced 'on the job', in opposition to the more holistic view presented in Chapter 1.

Visions of actual quality in education rely on an understanding that as a human and messy business one size never fits all, and this works at cross purposes with the neo-liberal desire to catalogue and standardise practice. Just as the teacher quality agenda has narrowed the definition of good teaching practice, so too has it narrowed the definition of effective professional development and learning, highly salient to the current discussion of facilitated practitioner inquiry as inquiry-based professional learning (Hardy and Rönnerman, 2011). We will return to this issue at a later point in this chapter.

The choice agenda

The final key tenet of neo-liberal ideology in education under consideration here is that of choice. Linked to accountability and teacher quality agendas through the argument for transparency in all things educational, the choice agenda argues for the privileging of market forces in education.

Transparency of educational outcomes, such that parents can make good choices about which schools are appropriate for their children has manifested in different configurations internationally. OfSTED reports and the associated league tables produced in the United Kingdom since 2005 were the first large-scale example of the choice agenda writ large. In the Netherlands, these figures are made public via

the National Education Inspection. The Commonwealth Government-owned MySchool.edu.au website in Australia was established in 2010 with the purpose of publishing information about 'school performance' in the public domain, and includes a comparison of schools' national testing results on a local and 'statistically similar schools' basis. The 'narrative of choice' (Mockler, 2013, in press) posits that transparency and 'data' are the keys to securing good education for children. As the national newspaper declared on the eve of the release of the website:

> For the first time Australian parents can see how their children's school is performing against its peers. For the first time they have the information they need to congratulate teachers who are helping their children to do their best and to put hard questions to those who are not.
>
> For the first time they have something more than word of mouth when it comes to deciding which school will give their children the best possible education.
>
> (A victory for everybody who believes in education, 2010)

In the context of Sweden and the Netherlands, the increasing ethnic segregation of schools as a partial product of immigration patterns over the past two decades has produced a range of social consequences for schools providing predominantly for students from ethnic minorities (Szulkin and Jonsson, 2007). The compromised educational outcomes as measured via traditional neo-liberal measures can be seen to have contributed to the constitution of these schools as less desirable for middle class students than their predominantly middle class counterparts, reinforcing this segregation as a by-product of choice.

The choice agenda has also manifested over time in the proliferation of school voucher systems, introduced at different points since the 1980s and '90s in countries including Sweden, the USA, Chile and Hong Kong. In many cases, school voucher systems, which allow parents to 'spend' their allocation of public funding on Government or non-Government schools for their children, have at their heart a deep distrust of public education and a philosophical commitment to the operation of principles of supply and demand in education.

Global education policy contexts and facilitated practitioner research

As noted in the introduction of this chapter, while none of these three policy agendas manifests directly in classroom practice (although increasingly we are seeing a 'joining of the dots' in some schools and classrooms where they can work to limit the scope of action and decision-making of teachers and students), they each highlight an important dimension of the context of teachers' work in the current age. The implications of the three policy agendas for classroom practice are highly significant, in that they increasingly encourage teachers to conceptualise their work in terms of what can be easily measured and quantified, and tend to value those things above the more complex, human dimensions of education practice. In practical terms, these policy contexts position some schools as highly capable of pursuing and maintaining partnerships for facilitated practitioner research, while others, trapped in the performance anxiety embedded in the realities of schooling in neo-liberal times, find themselves less capable of doing so. To return to the model presented in Chapter 1, in some contexts they can represent a limiting and constraining of the *lifeworld* by the *system*, while other school contexts are such that 'push back' is achieved against the policy, opening the door to the possibility of transformational partnerships.

Viewed together, these agendas also work to undermine the status of teacher professional judgement, which we argued in Chapter 1 and 2 is the core of good teaching, on the part of society at large and indeed, teachers themselves. The strong 'common-sense' logic that posits that teachers' judgement is somehow flimsy, suspiciously 'objective' or highly untrustworthy attacks its legitimacy, while the strongly competitive culture promoted by these agendas, on the part of both schools and individual teachers, makes the development and sharing of good judgement more difficult. Kemmis (2009) writes of the collective nature of truly critical (as opposed to technical or practical) action research, noting that it is 'undertaken collectively, by people acting together in the *first-person (plural)* as "we" or "us"' (p. 470, emphasis in original). The very act of engaging in critical or transformative practitioner research is thus to 'swim against the tide' of current global discourses in education.

Furthermore, in terms of university and school-based colleagues working together in facilitated practitioner research, it is worthwhile noting here that higher education is subject to its own set of consequences of neo-liberal ideology. For example, the ways in which teacher educators' work is 'counted' within the academy to privilege research whose impact can be clearly observed within rather than outside the academy itself can work as a deterrent to the kind of work we are focused on here. As such, to some extent, the development of generative relationships through facilitated practitioner research in schools relies on the goodwill and optimism of colleagues working across both 'sides' and a commitment to the development of praxis on the part of all. This issue of relationships will be expanded upon in Chapter 4 and further in Chapter 8.

It is important to note that for us, practitioner research in partnerships at its best should provide something of a foil to these discourses, across schools and universities, presenting the opportunity for teachers to build a shared understanding of their 'joint enterprise' (Wenger, 1998) and to problematise their practice rather than seek simple solutions to complex issues and dilemmas. Global education policy contexts, however, can be seen to impact upon the enactment of practitioner research such that it might be seen to have been variously subjected to 'co-optation or colonisation' (Cochran-Smith and Lytle, 1998: 21) at the hands of neoliberal agendas, in ways reminiscent of the colonisation of *lifeworld* by *system* referred to in Chapter 1.

National agendas and practitioner inquiry as a 'solution'

Nested within this global education policy context is a tendency on the part of governments to pose practitioner inquiry as a solution to some of the emerging questions and problems. In 2006, Stephen Kemmis reflected on the state of critical action research within the prevailing political context and observed that:

> Much of the action research that has proliferated in many parts of the world over the past two decades has not been the vehicle for educational critique we hoped it would be. Instead, some may even have become a vehicle for domesticating students and teachers to conventional forms of schooling.
>
> (Kemmis, 2006: 459)

The use of practitioner research as an implementation tool for education policy on the part of governments, including the appropriation of 'action learning' as a softer option than action research or practitioner inquiry (Groundwater-Smith and Mockler, 2009), sits largely behind Kemmis' observation. In this section, we explore an example of this from Australia, known as the Quality Teaching Action Learning project within the Australian Government Quality Teacher Program. This particular case has been chosen because it highlights the ways in which such projects might be used as implementation tools for Government policies rather than primarily vehicles for expansive professional learning and generative partnership.

Case: The Australian Government Quality Teacher Program (2000–2013) and Quality Teaching Action Learning (2003–2009)

Conceived of as a means for improving teacher quality, the Australian Government Quality Teacher Program (AGQTP) has existed in four different iterations since 2000. The Quality Teacher Program (2000–02) focused upon 'updating and improving' teachers' skills in the areas of literacy, numeracy, mathematics, science, information technology and vocational education in schools (Commonwealth of Australia, 2000). The Commonwealth Quality Teacher Program (2003–04) retained this disciplinary focus while adding to it the National Safe Schools Framework and the development and implementation of professional standards for teaching and school leadership (Commonwealth of Australia, 2003). In the 2005–09 iteration, the Australian Government Quality Teacher Program, the disciplinary focus had once again been broadened to include civics and citizenship, health education, languages and music (Commonwealth of Australia, 2005). In the project's most recent (and far smaller) iteration, where funding is provided only to projects catering for teachers working in the non-government sector, the parameters have been broadened once again to include environmental education for sustainability (linked to Science), geography and 'student wellbeing' (Commonwealth of Australia, 2010). Over the decade from 2000 to 2010, over \$305 million has been channelled into teacher professional development and learning through the various iterations of the AGQTP (Hardy, 2008; Commonwealth of Australia, 2010), through a vast array of professional development projects developed and administered by the state and territory Departments of Education and the various Catholic and independent school authorities.

The AGQTP is oriented towards teachers' individual and collective development. While there is some mention in the 2003 and 2005 editions of the guidelines of collaborative partnerships, the common emphasis across the projects is more in relation to content focus than to process. Nevertheless, the opportunity for school/university partnerships to be built in to AGQTP-funded projects existed, and was taken up in many cases through the expectation that school learning teams would engage an academic partner to support them in their work. In fact, the requirement within AGQTP-funded projects that no more than 15 per cent of the provided funding be spent on teacher release in some way fostered partnerships between individual academics and school-based colleagues as it provided an effective way to allocate the funding that could otherwise be notoriously difficult for schools to spend. Again, while inquiry-based professional learning was not a requirement of AGQTP-funded projects, the emphasis placed over the various iterations of AGQTP on professional learning that was situated, not representative of a 'one-off' approach, and sustained over time (Hardy, 2009) meant that contextualised, inquiry-based professional learning (and specifically 'action learning') became a preferred method.

Quality Teaching Action Learning: an AGQTP-funded project

A vast array of projects has been funded via AGQTP over its 11-year lifespan, and while these projects are loosely unified by their adherence to the aims and priority areas dictated by the meta-project, they are highly divergent and disparate in every other way. For this reason, it is useful to focus this discussion on a single large-scale project that ran over a number of years as part of the broader AGQTP project.

Quality Teaching Action Learning (QTAL) was administered by the New South Wales Department of Education and Training and offered to Government schools in NSW in four separate rounds over the course of the first three iterations of the AGQTP. Over the four 'rounds', 193 primary and secondary schools participated in the project, which gained almost $3 million of funding through AGQTP, with an additional $1 million contributed by participating schools out of local professional learning budgets.

QTAL was conceived of as a means of engaging teachers with and implementing the NSW model of pedagogy, known as Quality Teaching (NSW Department of Education and Training, 2003), which had been developed in the two years preceding the first QTAL round. Drawing on work on Authentic Pedagogy (Newmann and Associates, 1996) and Productive Pedagogies (Education Queensland, 2001), the Quality Teaching framework was commissioned by the NSW Department of Education and Training in 2002 with the intention of achieving system-wide implementation of pedagogical reform as quickly as possible. QTAL was seen as one means of achieving this broad saturation of Quality Teaching across NSW schools.

The professional learning strategy for the Quality Teaching Action Learning project involved:

- school-based projects to engage teachers in workplace learning that is based on a cyclic model of continuous improvement;
- provision for some clusters of schools to work in collegial networks;
- workplace mentoring and coaching aligned to meeting the NSW Institute of Teachers Professional Teaching Standards;
- flexible learning that includes components such as self-paced and facilitated online learning, face-to-face workshops, video and teleconferences, online mentors and discussion groups;
- local, regional and state workshops and conferences that enable participants to have their work publicly celebrated and critiqued;
- onsite and offsite participation in knowledge building and skill-sharing activities;
- partnerships with higher education institutions to provide expertise in the development, design and/or implementation of professional development activities (Ewing *et al.*, 2010: 4–5).

Each participating school was involved in one 'round' of the QTAL project, and over the four iterations of QTAL (2003–04; 2004–05; 2006–07 and 2008–09), the length of time allocated to the project became increasingly lengthened: schools involved in the 2003–04 or 2004–05 rounds were effectively allocated a maximum of 20 or 30 weeks (two or three school terms) respectively to complete their school-based project, while those in the final two rounds were afforded a far longer period of time to undertake their project: the 2006–07 project extended for four school terms, while the final round included capacity for schools to apply for funding for a further four terms.

QTAL schools were allocated an 'academic partner', whose role was to facilitate and support the action learning project, attending to the following suggested tasks:

- Conducting professional learning about the NSW Quality Teaching model
- Maintaining the focus on improving teacher professional learning
- Building understanding of the action learning processes
- Providing ideas and strategies for implementing action learning in the school context
- Encouraging interaction and sharing of ideas, feelings and experiences
- Documenting learning, e.g. by helping team members prepare progress and final reports (Bettison and Bradburn, 2006: 10).

Discussion of the role of the academic partner within the QTAL project will be expanded upon later in this chapter in the form of a second case study within the discussion of micropolitical contexts for practitioner inquiry.

While the QTAL project utilised an action learning approach, the focus of the project over its many iterations remained the broad implementation of the Quality Teaching framework in as many schools and classrooms as possible. While schools were able to fashion their local focus within these parameters, the reporting focus for each stage of the project emphasised the extent to which professional learning in relation to the NSW model of pedagogy had occurred and the extent to which this had changed classroom practice over the course of the project. In the final two iterations of QTAL, a 'scaling up' imperative was also emphasised within the project, where schools were asked to provide evidence that the professional learning and pedagogical change had expanded beyond the initial project team to other teachers within the school.

Developing transformational partnerships through large-scale funded projects

The funded project described above is by no means the only example of such work. In Australia, such projects have been 'rolled out' under the auspices of AGQTP as well as in other forms for the past two decades, and in other parts of the world similar projects have been funded on a national, state or province level in the name of implementation or 'improvement'. In England, for example, the now-defunct Master of Teaching and Learning practice-based degree, was initiated by the Brown Government in 2010 with the intention of using practitioner inquiry to support all teachers to 'gain the knowledge and skills they need to have a real impact in the classroom'(TDA, 2011). John Furlong adds that 'the ambitious hope of the [Master of Teaching and Learning] is that, by giving teachers opportunities to examine . . . national priorities for themselves, in their own classrooms, they will, over time, develop the personal commitment needed to make them effective' (2011: 117), suggesting that both 'upskilling' and implementation were the two dual aims of the project.

If we are to heed Carr and Kemmis' (2010) message about the central goal of critical action research as transformation of education and, ultimately, society, it seems that perhaps the role of the facilitator in large-scale funded projects is at least partly about supporting schools and teachers to 'serve two masters' in the enactment of their work. For while the funded project comes with resourcing to support professional learning, where it also comes with aims related to implementation of neo-liberal policy agendas, the potential for the work to become 'domesticated' comes to the fore. In the 2006 article used at the beginning of this discussion of national agendas, Kemmis went on to outline five categories of what he termed 'inadequate action research' (p. 460). Paraphrased, they are:

1   That which aims merely at improving techniques of teaching.
2   That which is aimed at improving the efficiency of practices rather than understanding the importance of context and consequence in social, cultural, discursive and material–economic historical terms.
3   That which is conducted with the sole purpose of implementing government policies or programmes.
4   That which does not engage with the voices or perspectives of 'consequential stakeholders' of the research.
5   That which is conducted alone rather than in open communication with others.

(Kemmis, 2006: 460–461).

It is not difficult to see that it might be possible to commit all five of these transgressions as a consequence of engaging in facilitated practitioner research in the context of a large-scale funded project: much depends on the particularities of the project itself as well as the capacity of the facilitator to support the project to 'move beyond' the parameters in local school contexts. To establish a dichotomy where the work can meet either the requirements of the project or the needs of the teachers involved is unhelpful, and the skilled facilitator can support practitioner researchers to elaborate their own desires in relation to the inquiry project and fashion an approach where local priorities are addressed, teachers are supported to engage critically and problematise their practice as much as the context of the project requires them to problem solve, while the external requirements are also met.

Micropolitical contexts

Nested within the global political context and the context of 'the project', which is often the field within which practitioner researchers engage in their inquiry, is the micropolitical context of the school and the research team, comprising both school- and university-based members. This local level is the immediate political context of practitioner research – we might think of the global policy context as the 'framing' context, the funded project as the contingent context and the local context as the immediate context.

As Eilertsen, Gustafson and Salo have argued (2008), action research has significant micropolitical implications that go beyond issues of conflict and power and impact upon, for example, co-operation and collaboration in the context of action research. A range of issues related to power and politics impact upon facilitated practitioner inquiry at this local level, some created by those broader contexts and some a product of the human interactions in the realm of *lifeworld* that are part of conducting collegial practitioner inquiry. Furthermore, these issues are usually ethical ones, linked to questions of ownership of research, conduct of research, reporting of research and so on. In terms of practice architectures, Kemmis has argued that the 'relatings' dimension of praxis, represented in the Aristotelian conceptualisation of 'ethics', is most closely linked to the social-political preconditions for practice, which can be seen to 'shape and give content to the "relatings" involved in the practice' (2006: 466). While 'sayings' and 'doings' are undeniably salient in the enactment of practitioner research, in terms of the micropolitical context, and particularly with reference to the transformational intent of critical practitioner research, we understand the 'relatings' to be of primary importance.

It should also be noted at the outset that the very act of facilitating critical practitioner research is a political one, insofar as the transformational intent itself is political, a means by which teachers might enter into professional renewal, explore and problematise their practice and engage in what Sachs (2000, 2003) has defined as 'activist professionalism'.

Micropolitics and the role of the facilitator

One of the key manifestations of the neo-liberal agenda within the school environment has been a decrease in the perceived value of teachers' professional knowledge and professional judgement. The associated 'deskilling' or 'deprofessionalisation' (Hargreaves, 1994; Hargreaves and Goodson, 1996; Helsby, 1998) of the teaching profession has been well documented over the past two decades. As noted above, a potent link exists, however, between practitioner research and teacher professional judgement, and to explore this we return to Stenhouse's notion of emancipation as the 'intellectual, moral and spiritual autonomy which we recognise when we eschew paternalism and the rule of authority and hold ourselves obliged to appeal to judgement' (1979: 163). For Stenhouse, the act of engaging with and honing professional judgement through practitioner inquiry itself held transformational and emancipatory power, and a key part of the role of the facilitator, we believe, lies in the fostering of confidence and capacity in the use of teacher professional judgement, grounded in robust professional knowledge: as we have argued earlier, action research constitutes a public deliberate rationality. To do so, however, is to challenge current orthodoxies, with their emphasis on that which is measurable and transparent, as opposed to that which is more messy and 'subjective', but despite the dominance of these ideas, we believe that the facilitation of transformative practitioner research demands it.

If supporting the building of professional judgement is a primary role of the facilitator, it is important to recognise the critical role of trust and rapport therein, and also to understand that within the micropolitics of the school, the building of trust and rapport between teachers and facilitators cannot be taken for granted. While in some school environments, a healthy expectation of reciprocity can be seen to exist at the outset, in others a variety of perspectives might be identified, from an expectation that the university-based colleague will bring 'the good oil' and must thus be deferred to, to 'ivory tower' assumptions that position potential facilitators as unaware of and uninterested in the realities of modern schooling. As with most educational phenomena, there is no recipe or set of instructions for navigating the micropolitics of schools when it comes to establishing trust and rapport. As experienced facilitators of practitioner inquiry across a broad variety of school and early childhood education contexts, we recognise the importance of approaching the school, as far as possible, without preconceived ideas as to how the relationship will unfold; of understanding the relationship as a *partnership* where all will bring valued expertise and engage in learning from each other. We also recognise the need to listen to local concerns and allow the focus of the practitioner inquiry to emerge from these rather than from our pre-conceived ideas about what should be done; of giving generously of our time and tailoring the process to the needs and desires of the teachers involved; and of gently subverting any of those above-mentioned prejudices that might be held within the school community, through attention, engagement and responsiveness.

One of the areas of expertise most likely to be brought to the practitioner research table by the facilitator and not necessarily part of the repertoire of the practitioner researchers at the outset relates to the area of research ethics. While teachers generally have a strong sense of professional ethics, support of professional learning in relation to ethical processes and procedures for research is often a key task for the facilitator. Elsewhere, one of us has written of this ethical dimension of practitioner research and the dilemmas that sometimes emerge out of the micropolitical context (Mockler, 2007). Indeed the development of practitioner researchers' understanding of ethics and power within the context of the practitioner research endeavour often sheds light on broader issues of professional ethics and classroom practice, and over time, can build significant 'cross-field effects' (Mockler, 2011b) in teacher researchers' practice, once again highlighting the transformative potential of practitioner research. The role of the facilitator in supporting the development of practitioner researchers' understanding and enactment of research ethics is thus framed by and can interact with the micropolitics of the school in a number of highly significant ways. The case reported below provides an illustration of this interplay.

Case: the role of the 'academic partner'

For this case study, we return to the context of QTAL. As noted in the earlier case study, a significant dimension of each school-based QTAL project was the alignment of the school (or, in some cases, cluster of schools) with an 'academic partner' who acted as a facilitator or 'critical friend' to the project. In most cases, the academic partner was a teacher educator appointed by the Project Managers, although schools could and did request individuals with whom they had formed a relationship in the past. In an attempt not to prescribe the nature of the relationship, the role of the academic partner was left for schools and partners to negotiate over the course of their relationship.

The 2010 meta-evaluation of the QTAL project (Ewing *et al.*, 2010) included an analysis of the role of the academic partner within the project across the 135 projects and four rounds of funding. It found that academic partners took on multiple roles over the course of the project (sometimes performing these simultaneously or in an integrated fashion), summarised in the following.

- *Academic partner as expert*: this role included the provision of 'expert knowledge' around either subject matter, the Quality Teaching framework, the Action Learning process or inquiry methods (or some combination of these), and included the provision of 'professional development' sessions and workshops, as well as ongoing support during and beyond team meetings.
- *Academic partner as mentor and critical friend*: this role essentially involved 'having a deep and profound understanding of the ways in which schools, as educational, social, and political enterprises operate' (Ewing *et al.*, 2010:

46–47), and possessing the capacity to bring this understanding to bear on the professional learning that was being undertaken within the project and expanding the learning as a consequence.

- *Academic partner as enabler*: this role encompassed the many strategies through which academic partners were seen to motivate, steer and facilitate teacher professional learning, such as via direct facilitation whereby teams were 'kept on track', the provision of resources and the encouragement of schools to develop their own resources as a consequence of the project.

'Outstanding' academic partners were seen to possess a quality and magnitude of professional knowledge that was both relevant to the project at hand and also 'translatable' into the local context. An understanding of how schools operate and a willingness to take a critical stance rather than to push a particular agenda were also seen as beneficial, as was a willingness to provide professional development for members of the project team as well as others within the school. In a sense, these 'outstanding' academic partners were those who routinely went 'above and beyond' the requirements of the project, to provide professional learning opportunities for teachers that were contextualised, timely and worked with concerns and priorities that emanated from the school itself. A willingness to give generously of their time such that they demonstrated a commitment to the school and project was also highly valued by school teams.

The 9 per cent of schools that expressed a level of dissatisfaction with the work of their academic partner focused largely on a mismatch of the partner's expertise with the needs of the school: a lack of time or capacity or willingness on the part of the academic partner to become truly connected to the school and thus be able to situate the learning they were facilitating within the life of the school, or a lack of clarity or need to further negotiate the role that the academic partner could or would play.

My own experience, as academic partner to one school cluster (comprising one secondary and three primary schools) and two secondary schools over three rounds of the QTAL project, resonates with these findings, but also to the importance of 'relatings' to the micropolitical context. While each of my three experiences was very different, I came to recognise that much about the team/academic partner relationship rested upon the prior experiences and general attitude of team members in relation to 'the academy'. At the time I was a relatively marginal member of the academic community, in that I was a part time PhD student who also ran my own educational consultancy and thus, in a sense, facilitation was my 'day job'. In the first instance, the school had formed a very generative relationship with an academic partner on a prior project, and they came to the QTAL process with optimistic expectations about what our relationship might look like and what I might be able to contribute. We each came to the task at hand in the spirit of genuine collaboration and joint enterprise, and over time built a highly successful working relationship that continued for many years after the end of the project. In the two subsequent 'rounds', my presence was met with a level of suspicion, a sense that academics lived in 'ivory towers' and were ill-informed of the realities of modern schooling. Over time these too developed into generative working relationships, to varying degrees, but in some ways, to the end of the relationship, the 'relatings' were coloured by these perceptions and my own responses to them, which caused me to think more of the associated projects as 'hard work' than the purely enjoyable and inspirational experience the first had been.

Conclusion

Each of the three nested political contexts described and elaborated here hold significant implications for the enactment and facilitation of practitioner inquiry. We do not suggest that each impacts in the same way across different school contexts, nor that each impacts in the same way across the course of a project. There are many internal variables that mitigate against and mediate the politics of practitioner inquiry; among them school culture and leadership, for example, and there is also a plethora of external variables that do the same, more or less powerfully depending on their prevalence in public discourse and the impact of that public discourse on the world of the school or school system. In this chapter we have aimed to demonstrate that not only is facilitated practitioner inquiry inherently political in that its very aim, to transform practice and schools, is itself intensely political, but also that the political context within which it is enacted is complex and multilayered. While the role of the facilitator is in some ways shaped by these politics, a key part of the facilitation process is related to anticipating and providing a foil to some of the more unhelpful political pressures: at times this can be about providing a counter-cultural voice or encouraging teachers to pause and ponder the orthodoxies of their community and society in the light of the provision of education for young people. At other times and in other contexts, this support might be enacted differently or less explicitly.

References

A victory for everybody who believes in education [Editorial]. *The Australian*, 30 January, 2010 p. 15.

Apple, M.W. (2001). *Educating the 'right' way: Markets, standards, god and inequality.* New York: RoutledgeFalmer.

Apple, M.W. (2006). *Educating the 'right' way: Markets, standards, god and inequality* (2nd edition). New York: RoutledgeFalmer.

Bettison, K. and Bradburn, K. (2006). *Quality teaching action learning project handbook.* Sydney: NSW DET.

Biesta, G. (2007). Why 'what works' won't work: Evidence-based practice and the democratic deficit in educational research. *Educational Theory, 57*(1): 1–22.

Carr, W. and Kemmis, S. (2010). Educational action research: A critical approach. In S. Noffke and B. Somekh (Eds) *Handbook of educational action research* (pp. 74–84). Thousand Oaks: Sage Publications.

Cochran-Smith, M. and Lytle, S. (1998). Teacher research: The question that persists. *International Journal of Leadership in Education, 1*: 19–36.

Commonwealth of Australia (2000). *Quality teacher program client guidelines 2000–2002.* Canberra: Department of Education, Training and Youth Affairs.

Commonwealth of Australia (2003). *Commonwealth quality teacher program: Updated client guidelines 2003.* Canberra: Department of Education, Training and Youth Affairs.

Commonwealth of Australia (2005). *Australian government quality teacher program client guidelines 2005–2009.* Canberra: Department of Education, Science and Training.

Commonwealth of Australia (2010). *Australian government quality teacher program client guidelines 2010.* Canberra: Department of Education, Employment and Workplace Relations.

Darling-Hammond, L. (2011). *The flat world and education, 2011 John Dewey memorial lecture.* Paper presented at the ASCD Annual Conference. San Francisco, CA.

Education Queensland (2001). *The Queensland school reform longitudinal study: Final report.* Brisbane: Education Queensland.

Eilertsen, T.V., Gustafson, N. and Salo, P. (2008). Action research and the micropolitics in schools. *Educational Action Research, 16*(3): 295–308.

Ewing, R., Groundwater-Smith, S., Mockler, N., Loughland, T., Simpson, A., Smith, D., Way, J., Armstrong, A. and Brooks, D. (2010). *Meta analysis of quality teaching action learning project.* Sydney: University of Sydney.

Furlong, J. (2011). The English masters in teaching and learning: A new arena for practitioner inquiry? In *Rethinking educational practice through reflexive inquiry* (pp. 105–119). Dordrecht: Springer.

Groundwater-Smith, S. and Mockler, N. (2009). *Teacher professional learning in an age of compliance: Mind the gap.* Dordrecht: Springer.

Hardy, I. (2008). Competing priorities in professional development: An Australian study of teacher professional development policy and practice. *Asia-Pacific Journal of Teacher Education, 36*(4): 277–290.

Hardy, I. (2009). The production of Australian professional development policy texts as a site of contest: The case of the federal Quality Teacher programme. *The Australian Educational Researcher, 36*(1).

Hardy, I. and Rönnerman, K. (2011). The value and valuing of continuing professional development: Current dilemmas, future directions and the case for action research. *Cambridge Journal of Education, 41*(4): 461–472.

Hargreaves, A. (1994). *Changing teachers, changing times: Teachers' work and culture in the postmodern age.* New York: Teachers College Press.

Hargreaves, A. and Goodson, I. (1996). Teachers' professional lives: Aspirations and actualities. In I. Goodson and A. Hargreaves (Eds) *Teachers' professional lives* (pp. 1–27). London: Falmer Press.

Helsby, G. (1998). *Changing teachers' work and culture*. Buckingham: Open University Press.

Kemmis, S. (2006). Participatory action research and the public sphere. *Educational Action Research, 14*(4): 459–476.

Kemmis, S. (2009). Action research as a practice-changing practice. *Educational Action Research, 17*(3): 463–474.

Mockler, N. (2007). Ethics in practitioner research: Dilemmas from the field. In A. Campbell and S. Groundwater-Smith (Eds) *An ethical approach to practitioner research* (pp. 88–98). London/New York: Routledge.

Mockler, N. (2011a). *The slippery slope to efficiency? An Australian perspective on school/ university partnerships for teacher professional learning.* Paper presented at the American Educational Research Association Annual Meeting. New Orleans, April 2011.

Mockler, N. (2011b). *When 'research ethics' become 'everyday ethics': The intersection of inquiry and practice in practitioner research.* Paper presented at the American Educational Research Association Annual Meeting. New Orleans, April 2011.

Mockler, N. (2013, in press). Reporting the 'education revolution': Myschool.Edu.Au in the print media. *Discourse: Studies in the Cultural Politics of Education, 34*(1).

Newmann, F. and Associates (1996). *Authentic achievement: Restructuring schools for intellectual quality.* San Francisco: Jossey-Bass.

NSW Department of Education and Training (2003). *Quality teaching in nsw public schools.* Sydney: NSW DET.

Ponte, P. and Ax, J. (2011). Inquiry-based professional learning in educational praxis: Knowing why, what and how. In N. Mockler and J. Sachs (Eds) *Rethinking educational practice through reflexive inquiry* (pp. 49–60). Dordrecht: Springer.

Ravitch, D. (2010). *The death and life of the great American school system: How testing and choice are undermining education*: Basic Books.

Rizvi, F. and Lingard, B. (2010). *Globalizing education policy.* Abingdon: Taylor & Francis.

Sachs, J. (2000). The activist professional. *Journal of Educational Change, 1*: 77–95.

Sachs, J. (2003). *The activist teaching profession.* Buckingham: Open University Press.

Sahlberg, P. (2004). Teaching and globalization. *International Research Journal of Managing Global Transitions, 2*(1): 65–83.

Sahlberg, P. (2007). Education policies for raising student learning: The Finnish approach. *Journal of Education Policy, 22*(2): 147–171.

Sahlberg, P. (2009). Educational change in Finland. In A. Hargreaves, M. Fullan, A. Lieberman and D. Hopkins (Eds) *Second international handbook of educational change* (pp. 1–28). Amsterdam: Kluwer Academic Publishers.

Steiner-Khamsi, G. (2004). *The global politics of educational borrowing and lending.* New York: Teachers College Press.

Stenhouse, L. (1979). The problems of standards in illuminative research. *Scottish Educational Review, 11*(1): 5–10.

Stobart, G. (2008). *Testing times: The uses and abuses of assessment.* Abingdon: Routledge.

Szulkin, R. and Jonsson, J.O. (2007). *Ethnic segregation and educational outcomes in Swedish comprehensive schools.* www.temaasyl.se/Documents/Forskning/Forskningsstudier/ Ethnic segregation and educational outcomes in Swedish comprehensive schools.PDF Accessed 30 July, 2011.

Taubman, P.M. (2009). *Teaching by numbers.* New York: Routledge.

TDA (Training and Development Agency for Schools) (UK) (2011). *Masters in teaching and learning.* www.tda.gov.uk/teacher/masters-in-teaching-and-learning. aspx Accessed 4 October, 2011.

Wenger, E. (1998). *Communities of practice: Learning, meaning and identity.* Cambridge: Cambridge University Press.

Chapter 4

Sustainability

Karin Rönnerman is the lead author of this chapter, and she was initiator of a course in action research for the development of quality in preschools in Sweden. Since its inception the course has been offered annually to early childhood teachers working in preschools in different municipalities. As this chapter demonstrates, the course has a number of specific characteristics that make it particularly interesting from a research perspective. Thus this chapter will, in particular, focus on the ways in which the development of transformative partnerships takes place in preschools by building on deeper knowledge, continuation over time, involvement of colleagues and the establishment of relations between teachers, principals, directors and researchers working together to sustain quality.

Introduction

This chapter examines the facilitation of practitioner research in ways that enable the critical dialogue and meaning making associated with transformative partnerships to be sustained over time. Facilitating practitioner research cannot be a 'quick fix' solution, rather it builds on a balance between *system* and *lifeworld* and also the ways in which the scope for autonomous action is developed within this balance. This chapter explores the concept of sustainability and argues that in the context of facilitating practitioner research it involves knowledge building focused on moral acting, and partnership relations that evolve in depth, length and breadth. To illustrate sustainable facilitation we will present a case from a long-lasting partnership that started with a course in action research for early childhood teachers and then evolved into networking and new challenges for both practitioners and researchers. Focus in this chapter will be on:

- how it is possible to develop and sustain partnerships that are originally created as coursework within a programme of study;
- how facilitation created within a course can be translated and built into a structure in local pre schools;

- how long-lasting partnerships can be developed between teachers and researcher, local authorities and a university, and how these can be sustained over time.

Sustainable development in education

Since the mid-1980s the concept of sustainable development has become a central feature of the worldwide political agenda. While there is a lack of consensus on the meaning of the concept, some definitions hold greater sway than others. As early as 1987, the World Commission on Environment and Development, the so-called Brundtland Commission, established the most authoritative definition:

> Sustainable development meets the needs of the present without compromising the ability of future generations to meet their own need.
>
> (WCED, 1987: 43)

While sustainable development is mostly connected to issues of environment, in the Brundtland report social as well as economic development is also included. Education has to handle the complexity and interdependence of all three dimensions of sustainability in its task of developing the skills and knowledge of new generations of citizens. In addressing the issues of environmental, social and economic development, questions often raised concern how an individual can make a difference by acting in particular ways, and how a more just and sustainable society can be achieved. Education can therefore be seen as the key for sustainable development, and learning a key for people to meet the challenges the world poses. UNESCO has proclaimed that development for sustainability should be highly prioritised in the period 2005–14, and has declared this to be a decade for Educational Sustainable Development (ESD). Initiatives to promote sustainable development should encompass the whole educational spectrum including early childhood education and also covering popular education across subjects, disciplines and continents (UNESCO, 2011). Education for sustainable development involves disseminating values and principles concerning equity, gender parity, social tolerance, poverty reduction, environmental protection and restoration, natural resource conservation and the development of just and peaceful societies. These values and principles can be aligned with the ideas mentioned in Chapter 2 as the basic values of freedom, equality and solidarity.

Seen in another way, sustainability is just a word and, as Scott and Gough (2003) argue, both meaning and perspective have to be related to the context in which the concept is implicated:

> 'Sustainability' is a word. Like all words, it relates to something outside itself. But like all words, its precise meaning is always dependent on the context in

which it is used. Given the possibility that we might eventually fail to sustain life on this planet, or at least diminish its richness, then there seems little of more importance than pursuing the debate about what we mean by this term, what we might mean, and what the adoption of such a meaning might lead us to do.

(Scott and Gough, 2003: 30)

Just like other words, we need to define the concepts that are represented when using them in a context different to that in which the term was originally used. Sustainability is just such a concept and, over time, has been developed and broadened to include more areas than the ones mentioned above. For example, Goodland includes a fourth area – *human* sustainability – that involves

the maintenance of human capital. Which includes health, education, skills, knowledge, leadership and access to services. Human is conceived as a private good of individuals.

(Goodland in Björneloo, 2007: 26–27)

The division of sustainability into different fields is not however without risks, as Scott and Gough (2003) point out. The point they make is that there is a risk that each field will just be developed within itself, having control over its own economy, with its own experts and with doors that are closed to other departments. This mirrors a reductionist way of thinking and a broader view on the problem is needed. Scott and Gough oppose attempts to find separate and demarcated solutions that purport to be sufficient for the global issues facing humankind, issues that include complexity, uncertainty and risks. Education becomes important and Scott and Gough encourage individuals and groups to create new ways of thinking and to expand beyond narrow perspectives and enclosed disciplines.

Our own claim would be simply that it is worthwhile, as a meta-level goal, to promote learning through enhanced awareness across individual, social, economic and environmental perspectives. Such learning would encourage individuals and groups to challenge the theoretical, practical, ideological and philosophical foundations of their thinking, while at the same time provide opportunities for them to share that thinking with others and to influence and learn from them. Clearly, to achieve this goal will involve discovering approaches to learning which appear acceptable in the first instance to a wide range of existing institutions, literacies and practitioners. It is no small challenge.

(Scott and Gough, 2003: 65)

The importance of providing opportunities for sharing time and for thinking with others, emphasised in the above quote, is also in line with the inter-subjective endeavour in partnerships discussed in depth in Chapter 2. For this task, Åhlberg (2005) argues, people with intelligence, wisdom and creativity are needed and he advocates collaboration between researchers and practitioners and, in particular, recommends action research for school development as a particular way forward. This is a perspective fundamental to the content of this book and also aligned with Blewitt's (2006) argument that sustainable development is a process oriented around dialogue:

> Sustainable development and its objective, sustainability, will come about through learning and reflecting on everyday assumptions, habits of behaviour, structures of feeling and expectation.
>
> (Blewitt, 2006: 3)

The above quote also accords well with the way in which the UNESCO programme for the decade (ESD) encourages the dismantling of traditional educational agendas and promotes one that emphasises: interdisciplinary and holistic learning (rather than subject-based learning); values-based learning; critical thinking (rather than memorising); multi-method approaches including the spoken word, art, drama, debating, etc.; participatory decision-making and locally (as opposed to nationally) relevant information.

One essential characteristic of sustainable development relates to the way that, as humans, we should conserve the planet for coming generations by acting responsibly during our lifetimes. This means focusing on human greed and the effects that this can cause in the long run and the sometimes devastating consequences that patterns of consumption can have for people. In dealing with these issues, education is charged with no small task. Teachers, principals, directors of education and researchers all have a specific role in taking all aspects of sustainability into account in professional practice, in developing sustainable education and in transforming partnerships. From this perspective, economic, social, as well as environmental issues need to be taken in to account. Priorities within the school budgets have to be made to support relationships with the universities as a means of enhancing knowledge by building partnerships. Since social and human issues might be taken for granted, they need to be put firmly on the agenda when choosing different forms of professional learning.

Based on this broad overview of the concept of sustainability we will elaborate on it by using the four concepts of *depth, length, breadth* and *relations,* in connection to the case of practitioner research partnership that will be presented in the next section. Depth is a determining factor for sustainability. By developing a professional practice, the practitioners' awareness of what they are aiming for by engaging in specific action for change increases, meaning that they become able to explain why they choose specific actions, how it enables children's development and learning and how it promotes their own professional skills. Depth is also connected to what is possible to achieve within a partnership, such as substantial knowledge built on dialogue. Length is a second determining factor for sustainability. Having sufficient time is a necessary precondition for developing practices that involve partnerships with academic partners. It needs to be a development that builds on knowledge that can be discussed and reflected on as opposed to a specific model developed externally by somebody else and then simply implemented. Time is needed for critically questioning actions and reflecting upon them, as well as for establishing relations in partnerships. The third determining factor is breadth of influence. The things practitioners do are of importance not only in their own classrooms but also in terms of how they can influence other practices in the school and connect to networks both within and across schools (as illustrated in Chapter 7). Alongside depth, length and breadth as concepts related to sustainability of practice is a fourth concept – relationships. In transforming partnerships we see relationships evolve among researchers and practitioners and linked to communication. The nature of relationships is a determining factor for the depth, length and breadth of the partnerships. As a frame for the case we use the concept of sustainability and refer to a moral and just way of acting that relates to depth, length, breadth and relations in transformative partnerships.

The case: building partnerships for sustainability

Acting for sustainability can be related to *system* and *lifeworld* that, as presented in the first chapter, each of us is a part of. In order to facilitate practitioner research, teachers, principals and researchers are dependent on systems in which policies work. As demonstrated in the previous chapter (Chapter 3) three political contexts – the context of global education policy, the national/regional context of large-scale funded projects and the local micropolitical context of the school and research team – all have an impact on the work to be done in school development that is built on partnerships between practitioners and researchers. Knowing and being aware of what these contextual features mean for the specific partnerships is of great help in understanding what can be accomplished.

Teachers, on the one hand, can be seen as bound by the political systems and varying governing bodies (such as, in Sweden, the National Board of Education) in terms of the ways in which they are expected to work in the classroom, as well as the types of professional learning programmes that are offered by the university. On the other hand teachers are not just passive marionettes, a picture easy to capture when talking about politics and *systems*. Systems can both enable and constrain their scope for action and decision-making. Teachers are professionals and have a responsibility to act for a just education for students. One way of developing this responsibility is through partnerships with researchers. The case presented below describes a course that was supported by funding from the Swedish National Agency for School Improvement and one of the national teaching unions. As a researcher I got the commission to develop this course for early childhood teachers and did so by establishing partnerships for facilitating practitioner research. The course was developed with close attention to teachers' experiences and professional knowledge and was initiated in 2004 as a course in action research for quality development in preschools. The course involved early childhood teachers from seven different local authorities in the western part of Sweden.

During the course year the teachers were divided into groups of eight (local school groups) and connected to a researcher from the university, whom they met eight times during the year to discuss and reflect on their research. In the design of the action research course two key factors were taken into account in order to ensure sustainability time and support. The first factor is related to the concepts of *depth* and *length*, which emphasised the importance of time for teachers to discuss and cement their ideas in their teaching teams; time to read the literature; time to conduct their research and time to build networks with teachers in other pre schools. Time became important here to enable teachers to deepen their knowledge. The second factor related to the concept *breadth* and encompassed awareness and support from the principals of the preschools. Breadth was emphasised, both in terms of the principals' purposes in sending teachers to the course and in terms of embracing the new knowledge and experiences that the teachers would bring back with them to the preschool on completion of the programme. To fulfil this purpose the principals were asked to invite the teachers who completed the course to participate in a seminar for all preschools in the local area in which their action research project would be presented and discussed with the teachers' peers (Rönnerman, 2008a). The researcher was also invited to this seminar.

Since its inception in 2004, the course has been used for developing quality work in preschools in a number of local authorities. Around 300 early childhood teachers have participated and long-lasting partnerships have been established during the years between the university and some of the local authorities. The results from a survey sent to 120 teachers five years after finishing the course, showed that the programme had been transformed into local practices for quality work (Rönnerman, 2008a). Eighty per cent of the teachers involved answered that they used action research and that it showed strength; as professionals they came to know and understand their professional practice more thoroughly through systematic inquiry and through research in partnerships for deeper knowledge (depth). It was also shown that 68 per cent of the teachers themselves over time started to facilitate action research with their colleagues in groups as a way to spread their knowledge further (length and breadth). Furthermore, relational work was emphasised by teachers, principals and co-ordinators in local authorities, and by the teachers and academics in the partnerships that were developed (relations). Here, partnership, with its collaborative and critical perspective, meant that through inquiry, meetings and discussions, teachers became aware of trends and policy shifts that were happening around them and could take an activist position by broadening their decision-making and their scope of action.

In order to focus further on the transformative partnerships, the next section will draw upon the aforementioned course for quality in preschools and discuss how the teachers involved in the course have sustained their work with action research by, for example, involving peers in the action research processes, facilitating peers and being facilitated by academic researchers (Rönnerman, 2008b). As we mentioned in Chapter 1, partnerships can be organised in different ways and for different purposes. In this case the partnerships between the university and local authorities started as a course in action research for early childhood teachers. The partnerships evolved over time and transformed into partnerships for practitioner research. Simultaneously, the partnership was also transformed into new networks within a number of the local authorities. In the next section this will be connected to the concepts of depth, length and breadth to illustrate partnership sustainability. The development of relationships between participants was also an essential part of the sustainability of the partnerships and will be examined later in the chapter using the concepts 'preserving', 'mutual empowerment', 'achieving' and 'creating a team' developed by Fletcher (1999).

Depth, length and breadth in partnerships

The intention of the action research course was to strengthen teachers' existing knowledge and at the same time to enable teachers to develop new insights that would encourage them to continue working with action research after the completion of the course. The aim of the course design was to move beyond the transactional idea of reading about and then applying theory to practice. Instead, the ideas prominent in the design of the course were to:

- emphasise knowledge derived from everyday life (experiences);
- improve each teacher's own workplace;
- collaborate with peers in practice development;
- integrate learning, development and improvement;
- establish groups for continued networking;
- establish a partnership with the university.

The most crucial part of the course was how to facilitate the groups of participants by a researcher. The process was structured in a particular way, the purpose being to make each step visible. Different tasks designed to encourage progression were used to fulfil and support the process. These tasks provided teachers with the opportunity to gain a grasp of action research as *functional rationality* (knowing how to do), as well as *substantive rationality* (knowing why and for what purpose). Both rationalities got attention in the design, and from that facilitation was carried out in such a way that it would:

- elucidate participants' expectations of the meetings;
- make visible different (practical and theoretical) perspectives;
- encourage participants to use their journals for individual reflection about facilitation;
- encourage awareness that all participants have equal rights to time and space;
- challenge taken-for-granted thinking;
- promote collegial (collective) reflection;
- establish connections between experiences and theories.

This design can now be related to our determining factors for sustainability. The *length* of the course – one year – during which the teachers were facilitated in groups of eight, was of great value. The teachers met the researcher once a month and facilitation was very much linked to what Lauvås and Handal (2001) among others call a 'critical friend' approach where the task is to challenge and develop the teachers' thinking as a means of enabling them to become aware of their praxis. To be a critical friend, with the purpose of presenting challenges, is a demand to both the researcher and the teachers in the group. Facilitation, by the researcher in this case, enabled teachers to collectively reflect upon specific aspects of the action research carried out in their own practice. Facilitation also enabled teachers to gain a deeper understanding, in that other views and perspectives were discussed based on research and theories that were ventilated in the meetings. This is expressed by one of the early childhood teachers:

> With help of analyses, reflection and ongoing discussions within the working team I notice that we are never satisfied. We have an ambition to be more sensitive to children's learning and development.
>
> (early childhood teacher)

In order to achieve reciprocity in partnerships, practitioners also needed to challenge the researcher and be critical about theories or research being discussed. It was necessary to create an atmosphere where practical as well as theoretical knowledge were acknowledged, where the meeting played an important role as a means of learning from one another and as a means of gaining a deeper understanding about how things work and how change can be brought about. The following quotation from one of the participants illustrates this point:

You have noted certain things in a new light, more consciously, and it has been a good source of discussing and improving your work.

(early childhood teacher)

To convey the idea that knowledge can be democratic, Gustavsson (2000) proposes using the Aristotelian division of knowledge in which practical knowledge can be valued as highly as theoretical knowledge. Such knowledge, possessed by people who are working in practice, is identified and characterised as 'familiar knowledge', 'tacit knowledge' or 'experiential knowledge', while academic knowledge is characterised as 'propositional knowledge'. By taking this into account, understanding can be deepened and sustained in practice involving everyday activities over time. In doing so the aspect of *depth* is fulfilled.

The third factor is *breadth*, which here is related to how the teachers' experiences and knowledge are drawn on to inform both other practitioners and the knowledge of the researchers:

I use new knowledge in my work with the children. Specifically I have improved through documentation. It becomes clearer and more structured. All teacher teams in five preschools work now the same way with action research. I facilitate them in groups of seven.

(early childhood teacher)

Facilitation and discussions in relation to your own actions make you go deeper into your work. It has also been helpful in my way of facilitating other teams.

(early childhood teacher)

The experience of this action research course seems to be that such partnerships are sustainable. Here it seemed that the creation of a structure was of particular importance in making it possible to both transform action research through facilitation into a local context, and to support further partnerships with the university. Teachers involved in these partnerships were involved in changing aspects of their practice, changing their understanding of practice and changing their understanding of the conditions within which that practice is undertaken (Carr and Kemmis, 1986: 165). Such changes served as a useful philosophical resource for affecting long-term, beneficial and sustainable teaching practice within the early childhood contexts and communication within the partnerships.

In relation to depth and breadth, another aspect to emerge from the project concerned how, through their own research and in using tools and holding meetings with the researcher, the teachers developed different kinds of knowledge (Rönnerman, 2005). This knowledge included, for example, forms of personal knowledge that developed through journal writing and personal insights; collegial knowledge that developed through critical dialogue, reflection and meaning making in the group with the facilitator and discursive and communicative knowledge that developed when practitioners talked about their work outside of their own immediate practice by, for example, presenting their projects at seminars, being active in study days and by writing a book together with me as the researcher (Nylund, Sandback, Wilhelmsson and Rönnerman, 2010). Representing such personal, collegial and communicative knowledge as an imaginary triangle, shows that the three kinds of knowledge meet. In this case they were interdependent in ways that extended the practitioners' knowledge base. This in turn enabled practitioners, building on their own experiences, to discuss and present their work in a wider sense to other colleagues and also in seminars at the university. Two particular examples serve to demonstrate how the course of action research was transformed into the local context, thus making quality work in preschools sustainable and demonstrating how transformative research partnerships were developed over time.

Example 1 – transforming facilitation into the local district

In the first example three teachers, all of whom participated in the first year the course was offered, worked in the same area but in different preschools. After finishing the course the teachers themselves acted as facilitators for their peers as a means of continuing locally with the action research. To be able to both cement the action research approach in the workplace and find time to meet, they used the time (two hours a week) for what, within the organisation, were called 'Pedagogical Mondays' – meetings composed of one person from each teaching team from the different preschools in which educational issues would be discussed. By building on this pre-existing arrangement, the teachers could more easily continue working with action research in their preschools by using this time for facilitation. Over the years it has developed and now all of the teachers (45 in total) from four different preschools have become involved. The three teachers who started facilitating their colleagues in 2005 not only continue to facilitate groups of their peers, but are also responsible for the content and structure of the compulsory study-day that takes place every August – a day that they use for planning quality work for the coming year based on issues that each teacher team identify (Rönnerman, 2008b). Furthermore, the three teachers also present their work in study-days for teachers invited to other local authorities, continue to meet the researcher for critical dialogue in groups, take part in seminars at the university, present lectures at the university (with the researcher) and together with the researcher, have written a book published by the national teaching union (Nylund et al., 2010) and have presented their work at a conference organised by the university. Their principals and the local authority with responsibility for running preschools who supported them by allocating time and, in this way, providing them with the legitimacy to facilitate their colleagues, enabled the teachers to further develop quality work. The teachers encouraged other teachers to become involved and extended their work so it could become something greater than their own individual practice. Looking more closely at the local context, it becomes apparent that the teachers, coming from three different preschools, had local conditions with a structure that made it possible to sustain their research and develop partnerships. Their work included all three concepts (depth, length and breadth) necessary for sustainability of the partnership and action research.

Example 2 – integrating facilitation into educational policy in the local authority

In the second example the quality co-ordinator in the local authority played an important role in integrating facilitation into local educational policy in sustainable ways. Three of the teachers who participated in the course in its first year were chosen by her to be mentors in the local authority where they worked. Their task was to facilitate teacher teams in action research in different preschools. In this example there was no pre-existing arrangement for the organisation of the research. The quality co-ordinator was therefore keen to get the action research cemented into the organisation and so established a committee that comprised herself, two principals and the three teachers with responsibility for the facilitation. This group not only provided knowledge for the quality co-ordinator regarding how the work on quality issues could be conducted, but was also a support for disseminating and cementing action research among the preschools in the local authority (Rönnerman, 2011). Interviews conducted with the co-ordinator revealed critical issues pertaining to the sustainability of the research partnership. The quality co-ordinator stressed the value of dialogue with the teachers. She mentioned that the teachers not only communicated the knowledge to the local authority board, but that they also had an important role in spreading awareness in other parts of the authority's educational provision such as, for example, to leisure time centres and schools. One important lesson learned from the teachers who facilitated other teacher teams concerned how to start to facilitate a group of teachers and the factors that need to be taken into consideration in order to ensure sustainability. It was not only the relationship between the teachers, principals and the quality co-ordinator that was of importance; cementing the approach in the preschool was felt to be equally as important. In one specific preschool action research was embraced as a procedure employed by individual teaching teams as well as within staff meetings. Within the teaching team action research was planned and carried out with the children. In addition the teachers also created their own 'quality group' within the preschool, which included a teacher representing each teacher team. This group was responsible for planning the work, critically discussing the chosen focus of the work, choosing ways of systematically gathering information as a basis for further inquiries and the development and responsibility for the annual quality audit. The staff meeting became an important arena for the four teaching teams at the preschool to meet and exchange experiences, as well as to reflect on their work and meet in critical dialogue. This example illustrates the ways in which time for critical dialogue was necessary at different levels.

At this preschool different forums and groups for critical dialogue and meaning making were established. These groups and forums included the four teaching teams, the group at the preschool with a representative from each team and the staff meetings. Furthermore, groups were established outside of the preschool groups, such as the mentor group with the quality co-ordinator, principals and two teachers from two preschools. All these groups ensured that action research was cemented throughout the organisation. This structure has stood the test of time and, seven years from its inception, is still sustaining teachers' work as mentors and partners with the university. The mentors and the quality co-ordinator have been presenting their work at the university and have frequently been requested to present it in other local authorities. Furthermore, the preschool itself has been involved in a collaborative research project together with me as the researcher in which the teaching teams constructed joint mind-maps with the researcher with the purpose of deepening their knowledge about their daily work (Rönnerman and Olin, 2010). Facilitating like this can be related to a second-person inquiry (Marshall, Coleman and Reason, 2011), which 'takes place when people work together face to face with others interested in issues of mutual concern' (p. 32). Such groups are comprised of individuals who, simultaneously, are both co-researchers and co-subjects. As co-researchers, members participate in thinking about how to frame the research, asking questions, choosing methods and making sense of experiences. This second example shows both depth (inquiries and critical dialogue in groups at different levels); length (seven years of practising facilitation); breadth (spreading among preschools) and a transformative research partnership built on relationships.

Partnerships as relational practice

The case above has exemplified the ways in which the three concepts of depth, length and breadth have been part of the sustainability of action research and the transformative partnership between the university, preschools and preschool authorities. In this last section of the chapter the three concepts will be linked to the relationships between partnership participants. In establishing sustainable partnerships, the relationships between all participants are one of the main issues that need to be taken into account. However, in education the concept of relationship is used primarily to talk about teacher–child interactions (Aspelin and Persson, 2011), and is rarely encountered in terms of teacher–teacher or indeed teacher–academic interaction. It is the children who are always mentioned first when teachers talk about what is important and what motivates them to continue as a teacher, and collegial relationships come second (see, for example, Hult, Olofsson and Rönnerman, 2006: 64). The work of organisation theorist Joyce K. Fletcher (1998, 1999), and in particular her reasoning about 'the relational practice of enabling others', will be drawn on to consider the course in action research and the part played by relationships in creating and transforming research partnerships and practice. In her action research project focused on gender equality among female design engineers in a building company, Fletcher talks about 'relational work' and shows how these aspects of work tend to disappear in favour of the dominant discourses in the workplace. In management literature, while teamwork, collaboration and learning are all emphasised, Fletcher nevertheless asks:

> Why is it that although there is an espoused organisational belief in collaboration and supportive teamwork, people who exhibit such behaviour seem to get disappeared from the organizational screen?
>
> (Fletcher, 1999: 3)

Her question is also relevant for an educational context in which, although highly emphasised, collaboration and teamwork is almost never discussed or recognised when talking about developing teachers' professional learning. In these discussions it is policy issues and learning outcomes in relation to international testing that tend to be prioritised. Fletcher makes the point that it is important to distinguish between to *be* invisible and to be *made* invisible. The latter, she argues, is influenced by 'Systems of practices, norms and common understandings' (p. 3). This reasoning can also be connected to what, in Chapter 1, we refer to as *system* and *lifeworld*. In the action research course discussed in this chapter, one of the striking effects concerned how the teachers talked about the importance of their collaboration with others in continuing with practitioner research and facilitating peers, as well as the desire to continue with the partnerships and to develop them further. This is something the teachers believed in and continued to do, and not something that was imposed upon them by others or that was written into a policy that they were required to implement. It was made visible. One of the teacher-facilitators puts it like this:

> Three of us from our school area attended the course together. We have divided all teacher teams from three preschools into three mixed groups. We meet and facilitate them four times during a semester.
>
> (teacher facilitator)

In a way the teachers stretched the borders of their teaching practice by enlarging the scope of action. The teachers' practices were supported in different ways both by the principals and the university researchers through their provision of opportunities to show others how action research works and to argue for its depth, length and breadth. It is, as one of the teacher-facilitators put it, a question of:

> having follow-ups with the principal when we discuss how our work is proceeding.
>
> (teacher facilitator)

The relations with others are important for this to happen and to ensure that such collaboration is durable. In her study Fletcher (1999: 169 ff.) identifies four different categories of relational practices. These are: *preserving*, which is associated with the task and aims to keep the commission alive and make it easier to carry it through; *mutual empowering*, which refers to making it possible and to strengthening others in their work in fulfilling the task and supporting the development of others; *achieving*, which is about strengthening professional development and effectiveness and making it possible to achieve goals and to contribute to the progress of the project and, finally, *creating a team*, which refers to creating good conditions for the team so that positive results are obtained for both the individual and the group. Among other things this has to do with acknowledging each others' knowledge and experiences.

Although Fletcher's study focused on a team from a profession different to teaching, the categories she maps out nevertheless are useful when focusing on education. The teachers involved in the action research course discussed here talked about the importance of collaboration and relations to others. They mentioned both their colleagues, as well as the contact with the researcher as a means of sustaining a living dialogue and disseminating knowledge about action research to their peers. This is closely allied to the element of *preserving* in Fletcher's model. The teachers took on a leading role and facilitated groups of colleagues from different preschools. They also contacted the university to create new meetings in which the researcher can facilitate them, not just in terms of their own action research, but also in their role as a facilitator of their peers pertaining to ways of developing critical dialogue and an inquiring culture. Other examples of how relationships have developed in the partnerships include the way in which the university has invited the teachers to seminars and conferences so that they can present their work to the academy, and, conversely, how the researcher has been invited to the local authority to talk about action research. This could also be viewed as *mutual empowerment*. In transformative partnerships it is about strengthening each other's position by building and enhancing the relations. This is done through collaboration and merges into the third category of *achieving*.

There is evidence from the teachers regarding the ways in which the participation in the action research has contributed to their professional learning and strengthened their practice both during and after the course. In particular teachers talked about how certain tools and the process of being facilitated by a researcher have been important for their professional development:

> In different ways, she [the researcher] has helped us to gather our thoughts. She has been a sounding board. She has helped us to organise our thoughts and has helped us to concentrate and focus on important issues for our own development and our engagement with children.
>
> (early childhood teacher)

We can also refer our cases to the final category mentioned by Fletcher; *creating a team*. In the example described in Chapter 6, as well as in the current example, this is something the teachers explicitly recognise. In some of the preschools the principal has been highly instrumental in shaping conditions that are conducive for the teachers to continue with practitioner research. In these contexts the principal has been fully aware of the value of the teachers' work. In working towards the children's learning and development, a balance between the individual and the collective characterises the collaboration within the team.

Beyond facilitation: summary and conclusion

In this chapter the case presented was a year-long course in action research offered for early childhood teachers. The course involved a university researcher working in partnership with preschool teachers in local groups. How the transformative partnerships became sustainable is shown primarily through the way in which the course developed and was cemented within the local authorities. In terms of *depth* we can see how the teachers deepened their knowledge by carrying out enquiries in their own settings, through discussing and reflecting on data together with researchers. This was not only done as part of different activities but also involved critical discussion regarding purpose and the need to ensure a socially just development for young children. In terms of *length* this development can be seen in the year-long action research course in which facilitation of groups of teachers was a central part. The teachers in their everyday work extended the action research by facilitating peers and maintaining contact with the university. Finally, *breadth* can be seen in the way the teachers have taken up new knowledge and invited other teachers into groups that they facilitate. Furthermore, the three aspects are visible in the way in which relationships between people, and relations across institutions, have been developed and maintained. Contact with the university researchers has continued, teachers have taken on new roles of facilitation with peers, and, finally, other teachers have been invited to participate in seminars and joint conferences organised by the university. Indeed, strong and ongoing networks have been established within the local authorities and between the local authorities and the university. Building on the experiences from the course and its specific way of developing transformative research partnerships, a new masters programme was established at the university, starting in 2011.

In this chapter relationships have also been emphasised as important in transformative partnerships. While at the outset of the course the relationship between and among the teachers and the researcher was formal, this has changed over the years and developed into something else. First, the teachers enrolled on the programme have transformed the facilitation they themselves have been a part of into long-term partnerships for quality enhancement in which they are active in facilitating their own peers (Edwards-Groves and Rönnerman, forthcoming). Second, the relationship between the university and the preschools has expanded and developed into an equal partnership. Together with the researcher, the teachers give lectures about the work that they have conducted within the preschools. The teachers have also challenged the researcher by asking about ways in which the work can be continued. It is noticeable that the meeting between the two fields of knowledge (practical and theoretical) has turned in to a 'communicative space' (Kemmis, 2007, see also Chapters 2 and 6) in which issues that are discussed and reflected upon provide meaning and shared understandings of practice. In this way, this particular course of action research has demonstrated that with the passing of time participants sought to go beyond simplistic decontextualized 'what works' (see, for example, Biesta, 2007) approaches to ones where they more carefully considered how best to address the difficult work of challenging accepted practices in order to develop conditions that can genuinely enrich teachers' learning, rather than simply managing them through fixed solutions. This chapter has demonstrated how a course in action research developed professional learning (depth), continued over time (length), spread knowledge to other professionals (breadth) and built relationships for transformative partnerships. Linking this to Figure 1.1 presented in Chapter 1, this case illustrates a balance between *system* and *lifeworld* and also between *substantive* and *functional rationality* in the ways in which teachers can broaden their scope for action and decision-making. In the last chapter we will elaborate on this further.

References

Åhlberg, M. (2005). *Educating for wisdom, creativity and intelligence as a main part of Education for Sustainable Development.* Paper presented at the Fifth Conference of ESERA (European Science Education Research Association). Universitat Pompeu Fabra, Barcelona, Spain, 28 August 28–1 September, 2005.

Aspelin, J. and Persson, S. (2011). *Om relationell pedagogik.* [About relational practice.] Malmö: Gleerups.

Biesta, G. (2007). Why 'what works' won't work: Evidence-based practice and the democratic deficit in educational research. *Educational Theory, 57*(1): 1–22.

Björneloo, I. (2007). Innebörder av hållbar utveckling: En studie av lärares utsagor om undervisning. [Meanings of sustainable development: A study of teachers' statements on their education.] *Göteborg: Acta Universitatis Gothoburgensis* [Göteborg studies in educational sciences], p. 250.

Blewitt, J. (2006). *The ecology of learning. Sustainability, lifelong learning and everyday life.* London: Earthscan.

Carr, W. and Kemmis, S. (1986). *Becoming critical: Education knowledge and action research.* London: Falmer Press.

Edwards Groves, C. and Rönnerman, K. (forthcoming). Generating leading practices through professional learning. *Journal of Professional Development.*

Fletcher, J.K. (1998). Relational practice: A feminist reconstruction of work. *Journal of Management Inquiry, 7*(2): 163–186.

Fletcher, J.K. (1999). *Disappearing acts: Gender, power and relational practice at work.* Cambridge, London: The MIT Press.

Gustavsson, B. (2000). *Kunskapsfilosofi: Tre kunskapsformer i historisk belysning.* [Knowledge: Three different forms in a historical view.] Stockholm: Wahlström and Widstrand.

Hult, A., Olofsson, A. and Rönnerman, K. (2006). *Tio år senare – Lärares syn på yrket i en skola under förändring.* [Ten years later – Teachers' view on their profession in a school of change.] *I Länsförsäkringar: Lärarrollen i ett föränderligt samhälle.* [Teaching profession in a changing society] (pp. 43–70). Falun: Intellecta.

Kemmis, S. (2007) Participatory action research and the public sphere. In P. Ponte and B.H.J. Smit (Eds) *The quality of practitioner research.* Rotterdam: Sense Publishers, pp. 459–476.

Lauvås, P. and Handal, G. (2001). *Handledning och praktisk yrkesteori.* [Facilitation and praxis.] Lund: Studentlitteratur.

Marshall, J., Coleman, G. and Reason, P. (Eds) (2011). *Leadership for sustainability. An action research approach.* Sheffield: Greenleaf Publishing.

Nylund, M., Sandback, C., Wilhelmsson, B. and Rönnerman, K. (2010). *Aktionsforskning i förskolan – trots att schemat är fullt.* [Action research in pre school – thus a full schedule.] Stockholm: Lärarförbundets förlag.

Rönnerman, K. (2005). Participant knowledge and the meeting of practitioners and researchers. *Pedagogy, Culture and Society, 13*(3): 291–311.

Rönnerman, K. (2008a). *Medvetet kvalietsarbete. En uppföljning av kursen Q i förskolan och dess inverkan på förkollärares handlingar i praktiken.* [Conscious quality work. A follow up of a course in preschool and its effect on acting in practice.] IPD-rapporter, 7. Göteborg: Göteborgs universitet, institutionen för pedagogik och didaktik.

Rönnerman, K. (2008b). Empowering teachers. Action research in partnership between school and university. In K. Rönnerman, K. Moksnes, E. Furu and P. Salo (Eds) *Nurturing praxis: Action research in partnerships between school and university in a Nordic light* (pp. 157–174). Rotterdam: Sense Publishers.

Rönnerman, K. (2011). Aktionsforskning – kunskapsproduktion i praktiken. [Action research – building knowledge in practice.] In S. Eklund (Ed.) *Lärare som praktiker och forskare – om praxisnära forskningsmodeller.* [Teacher as practitioner and researcher – about practice based research models.] (pp. 50–63). Stockholme: Stiftelsen SAF i samarbete med Lärarförbundet.

Rönnerman, K. and Olin, A. (2010). *Learning for leading: Mapping teachers' 'sayings' about acting in practice.* Paper presented within the symposium Leading, Learning and Ecologies of Practices: International Perspectives at Australian Association for Research in Education (AARE) Conference. Melbourne, 29 November–2 December.

Scott, W. and Gough, S. (2003). *Sustainable development and learning. Framing the issues.* London: RoutledgeFalmer.

UNESCO (2011). *Education.* www.unesco.org/new/en/education/ Accessed 20 October, 2011.

WCED (World Commission on Environment and Development) (1987). *Our common future.* London: Oxford University Press.

Chapter 5

Professional learning

Jane Mitchell is the lead author of this chapter. Jane has a long standing interest in the relationship between research and practice, and so the opportunity to build partnerships between schools and universities has always been a professional goal. Along with all authors of the book, Jane has been involved in a number of professional learning projects with schools that have employed practitioner research. This chapter draws on the collective work of all authors to set the scene for understanding professional learning partnerships between schools and universities. The chapter then presents two cases in which Jane was involved that illustrate ways in which practitioner research can be facilitated as part of professional learning programmes.

Facilitating professional learning

Action research and practitioner research are widely advocated as mechanisms that support professional learning for teachers. As previous chapters of this book have illustrated, researching aspects of one's classroom practice provide important means of building knowledge in ways that inform professional learning and hence practice. The aim of this chapter is to explore the means by which practitioner research can be facilitated as part of planned programmes of professional learning for teachers and as part of partnership between universities and schools. The chapter reviews two cases of innovative practitioner research partnerships between schools and universities to illustrate aspects of the facilitation process, how facilitation supported professional learning and knowledge building in both school and university contexts, and some of the opportunities and challenges associated with practitioner research facilitation.

The questions guiding this chapter are: How can practitioner research be facilitated in ways that support professional learning for all partners? What forms of facilitation of practitioner research best support teacher professional learning? What knowledge do facilitators need and how is that knowledge developed?

A central premise of the chapter is that the facilitation of practitioner research can be crucial to the nature and type of professional learning for practitioners. Moreover, when facilitation is conducted as a partnership between teachers and university faculty, there is potential for considerable professional learning for all partners in ways that transform the teaching and research practices within schools and universities.

This chapter is located within two sets of research literature – the literature related to professional learning and the literature related to practitioner research conducted by teachers. There are strong points of overlap between these two sets of literature because of the ways in which practitioner research is seen as a type, or form of, teacher professional development or learning (Rönnerman, 2005; Rust, 2009); and more specifically because of the ways in which the processes of practitioner research often align with what the literature has identified as productive forms of teacher professional learning (Groundwater-Smith and Mockler, 2009; Cochran Smith and Demers, 2010). There is general recognition in the literature that productive professional learning is: connected to teachers' classroom and work contexts; developed over the long term rather than through 'one-off' models; conducted within professional communities and underpinned by relevant research (Hoban, 2002; Mockler, 2005; Webster-Wright, 2009). Common conceptualisations of practitioner research, with its focus on inquiry and knowledge building related to practice; cycles of action and reflection; processes of collaboration and concern to change, improve and transform practice, provide the means by which the above features of professional learning can be materialised (Groundwater-Smith and Mockler, 2009). Such links between practitioner research and teacher learning are now commonly embedded as part of school policy related to professional development and learning (Furlong, 2005). However, as Chapter 3 in this volume notes, the politics underpinning policy are not fixed and much advocacy is required to sustain and support professional learning partnerships based on practitioner research.

Rust (2009) extends the link between practitioner research and professional development by arguing that teacher research provides a mechanism for 'bridging the gap between academic research and knowledge derived from practice' (p. 1886). Rust furthers this idea by suggesting that professional development should provide the opportunities to bring research and practice together. The points raised by Rust connect to our concern raised in Chapter 1; the means by which the facilitation of practitioner research partnerships can close the gap between scientific knowledge and practitioner-based knowledge. Moreover, Rust's idea of the bridge between academic research and practitioner research certainly links to ideas about school–university partnerships and, more specifically, how models of professional learning can be developed in order to connect different types of research knowledge and apply that knowledge in meaningful ways to educational practice.

There has been considerable advocacy of university–school partnerships that work to support teacher research, the development of practice-based knowledge and links to academic research (Grundy and Robinson, 2004). Within such partnerships the university partners are typically seen as the providers of expertise related to forms and methods of practitioner research. These forms and methods are subsequently employed by teachers as a means of understanding and refining practice in schools. The epistemological foundations for practitioner research methodologies have a strong link to conceptual and methodological work undertaken in universities (e.g. Carr and Kemmis, 1986; Schön, 1987, 1991; Loughran, 2003; Kemmis, 2009; Ponte and Ax, 2011). While recognising the expertise held by those working in universities, much of the partnership literature, along with the literature on practitioner research, acknowledges the expertise held by teachers in terms of their pedagogical and practice-based knowledge and skill. Partnerships between universities and schools thus often represent an opportunity for joint forms of practitioner research, two-way knowledge exchange and professional learning for all partners across institutional boundaries (Mitchell, 2007; Mitchell, Hayes and Mills, 2010).

Within the literature related to school–university partnerships there is much that distils the practices that support teacher professional learning and the sustainability of practitioner research partnerships. In a review of two partnerships programmes Erickson, Minnes-Brandes, Mitchell and Mitchell (2005), for example, note the following as key to achieving aims related to enhancing understanding of classroom practice and developing models of professional learning: mutual understanding of good teaching; teacher responsibility for direction of the research and regular meetings between teachers and teacher educators that help to support trust and good relationships. While recognising the above as important components of school–university partnerships, the specific means by which teacher research is facilitated by university faculty in order to support professional learning is less well documented in the literature (Poekert, 2010). In acknowledging this gap in the literature Poekert calls for a 'pedagogy of facilitation' related to teacher research. In investigating aspects of the facilitation of teacher research Poekert has identified some components of this pedagogy. The components include: moving beyond the logistics of project completion to meaningful reflection; varying the facilitation methods depending upon the stage of the project and in ways that scaffold teacher learning and the provision of both individual support and group collaboration. Lendahls Rosendahl and Rönnerman (2006) make the important point that the value of school–university partnerships for teacher professional learning is often assumed. Their study highlighted three 'tensions' regarding roles, purposes and relationships associated with the facilitation of partnerships and professional learning. These tensions pertain to the 'divergent' expectations of the different partners; the 'legitimacy' of the university role; 'weaknesses' associated with communication and the development of a common sense of purpose. The above findings are useful in that they begin to explicate components of the facilitation process, and its problems and possibilities, in relation to achieving goals related to partnerships, research and professional learning.

It is of note that there is much professional learning through practitioner research that occurs outside of formal partnerships, or in ways not completely dependent on partner input and facilitation, as demonstrated in Chapters 2, 4 and 6. Clearly, there are questions related to the ways in which such research is facilitated. However, this chapter will focus specifically on the facilitation of practice-based research developed as part of formal partnerships between schools and universities and the implications that this has for professional learning. This chapter also draws on case studies in which the university partner had responsibility for facilitation. While the ideas developed in this chapter will focus on university-led facilitation, they will also have relevance to facilitation conducted outside of formal partnerships and by a range of personnel.

Key concepts

Chapter 3 demonstrated the complex micro- and macropolitics that can underpin practitioner research partnerships. Embedded in these politics are sets of discourses at policy or system level for schools and universities, and at a local school and university level. These discourses pertain to research, teaching, professional learning and partnerships (Mitchell, Hayes and Mills, 2010). Often the discourses that frame practice at universities at a local and policy level can simultaneously complement and contradict those governing the operation of schools and school systems. For example, while there is often talk of school–university partnerships for the purposes of professional learning at a policy level, they can be hard to constitute at a local level because of competing assumptions, models and resources pertaining to professional learning.

Likewise, within institutional sectors, the discourses related to system policy can both contradict and complement the local level discourses. For instance, the policy discourse related to research processes, outputs and publications in universities at a system level is often very different to local level discourses within faculties of education that honour practitioner research and its relationship to teaching practice in school and university settings.

These sometimes competing, and sometimes aligned, discourses can create a partnership tension between universities and schools that impacts on the potential for practitioner research, professional learning and exchange across institutional boundaries. Professional learning for all partners can be most productive when there is close alignment or overlap between school and university discourses at a local and policy level (Mitchell, Hayes and Mills, 2010). Identifying how such professional learning partnerships can be facilitated is therefore crucial.

The above ideas can be linked to the notion of praxis and practice architectures (Kemmis and Grootenboer, 2008; Kemmis and Smith, 2008 raised in Chapter 1) in the following ways: policies framing teacher professional learning and teachers' work in school systems, and policies framing research and the work of academics in universities, constitute the 'meta-practices' in which individuals in schools and universities can develop partnerships and undertake practitioner research. These meta-practices, and their cultural, economic and political underpinnings, vary in terms of their conduciveness to partnership relationships and mutual knowledge building. Individuals within schools and universities traverse and transform these meta-practices at local levels through partnership arrangements and the 'sayings', 'doings' and 'relatings' that constitute the partnerships. Identifying the 'sayings', 'doings' and 'relatings' within partnerships related to practitioner research and professional learning provides a means of examining how and why such partnerships are facilitated. Table 5.1 provides some ways of framing components of the professional learning partnerships between schools and universities.

Table 5.1 Partnership practice architectures

Professional learning, partnership and research meta-practices pertaining to schools and universities

Facilitation practices	Schools	Universities
'Sayings' within the cultures of schools and universities	• What teachers say about universities and partnerships	• What university faculty say about schools and partnerships
	• What teachers say about professional learning and practitioner research	• What university faculty say about professional learning and practitioner research
'Doings' within the economics of schools and universities	• What teachers do in professional learning partnerships	• What university faculty do in professional learning partnerships
	• What practitioners do to undertake research	• What university faculty do to facilitate practitioner research
'Relatings' within the social and political contexts of schools and universities	• How roles and relationships are developed within partnerships	• How roles and relationships are developed within partnerships
	• How relatings between people, practices and concepts are made possible through facilitation	• How relatings between people, practices and concepts are made possible through facilitation

This chapter will describe some of the sayings, doings and relatings associated with facilitating practitioner research and professional learning partnerships in order to identify ways in which such research and learning can transform practice. Facilitation provides a key for making connections between research and practice; for bridging the institutional policies and practices of schools and universities and subsequently for professional learning and the transformative possibilities located therein. Through a consideration of two cases, the chapter will particularly focus on the process of facilitation in partnerships that enabled practitioner research and the associated professional learning within both school and university contexts.

Facilitating professional learning case studies

As other chapters have demonstrated, there are many ways in which the facilitation of practitioner research in transformative partnerships can occur. This section of the chapter will examine two cases in which the author has worked with teams of university-based practitioners to facilitate practitioner research as part of partnership arrangements between schools and university faculty. The cases will illustrate the ways in which facilitation occurred and how it supported research and professional learning. The cases will then be considered in light of the concepts outlined in Table 5.1.

Case one: facilitating professional learning as part of postgraduate study

Cohort-based programmes in which groups from one institution embark on a common course of postgraduate study are a relatively small part of programmes of study in faculties of education, yet they contain considerable potential in relation to building research-based knowledge and creating professional learning opportunities that bridge the gap between research and practice, and between universities and schools. This case is based on a cohort of 30 secondary school teachers from one school who enrolled in a Master of Education degree at their local university. The number of teachers, and the creation of a formal partnership arrangement between the school and the university, enabled the programme to be run at the school. Coursework for study by the cohort was carefully selected and delivered in order to meet the specific needs and interests of the teachers.

The main reason the school developed the partnership with the university, and why teachers enrolled in the course, was to build professional knowledge relevant to working with students from refugee backgrounds, many of whom had a severely interrupted experience of school. The course-based masters involved three content strands – pedagogy, curriculum and professional learning.

Assignment work included practice-based research within the teachers' class-rooms and school environment.

A core task for the university team involved with this programme was to facilitate postgraduate study in ways that supported participating teachers' professional learning, and in ways relevant to the teachers' classroom practice. Facilitation in this context encompassed the establishment of the partnership and negotiation of a cohort-based programme and course content; the design of subjects to meet local need; face-to-face teaching of each part of the course at the school site through lectures, seminars, presentations, etc. and the assessment of student work. In all subjects undertaken the teachers were required to make connections between published research and their own practice. In a number of subjects the teachers also completed tasks that involved classroom inquiry or research. This classroom-based research included developing and evaluating teaching resources; collecting and analysing classroom data and writing detailed reflections on specific aspects of their own and others' classroom practice.

This school–university partnership had a number of important and interesting features that related to the facilitation of professional learning and the relationship between school and university partners. There was a relatively long time frame for the partnership in that it extended over a three-year period of part-time study. Because the programme of professional learning was linked to a university credential, participants needed to meet assignment requirements set for postgraduate study. The focus on university study enabled participants to access and use varied forms of educational research. Programme participants read and reviewed research published in academic books and journals. Likewise, participants planned and undertook practitioner research projects in their own school and classroom as part of their assignment work. In many respects programme participants adopted a new role; they were students reading research and researching their practice, as well as teachers.

The classroom-based research components of the course were extremely important for the teachers. It provided them with opportunities to develop and trial teaching resources and in so doing explore pedagogical approaches useful in their classrooms. Likewise, the focus on classroom research enabled participating teachers to develop skills related to the collection and analysis of data, as well as to conduct detailed reflection on aspects of their pedagogical practice. In so doing the programme enabled participants to engage in sustained professional learning related to their workplace.

Opportunities to be involved in facilitating such a programme are rare and rewarding. They also contain numerous challenges. Perhaps one of the biggest facilitation challenges related to the course curriculum, and in particular to thinking about ways in which different types of research (practitioner research and academic research) could be incorporated into course content and course assignments in ways that met teachers' practical professional learning needs. An underlying 'saying' of the course was that research in all its forms is useful for teachers. A key facilitation question that emerged was: In what ways could academic research related to curriculum and pedagogy be made meaningful to the day-to-day practices of teachers? This question was particularly difficult to address because there was relatively little research related to the specific peda-gogical issues facing secondary school teachers working with students who had limited experience of schooling. The existing research was often only partially or tangentially relevant to the immediate needs of teachers.

The above problem led to a second facilitation question: In what ways could practitioner research provide a means of building knowledge relevant to the prob-lems of practice faced by teachers? Alongside this question was an additional dilemma: How could the practitioner research conducted by teachers be completed in ways that met assessment standards for a postgraduate qualification? The facili-tation therefore needed to acknowledge that the teachers were, in many respects, best placed to articulate new pedagogical knowledge through their research. At the same time, the research conducted by teachers needed to be located within the academic research literature in order to meet university assignment require-ments. Facilitation therefore required the development of bridges between the academic literature and the outcomes of teachers' own inquiries. While this bridging was a 'facilitation ideal', my own practices in this respect were often faltering as the language, time frames, foci and priorities of academic research and school and classroom practice were not always neatly aligned. Writing assign-ments seemed a long and lengthy process compared to the immediacy of the pedagogical practices in classrooms. Research published in many of the academic journals seemed to talk about educational practices in ways far removed from the teachers' daily work. Bridging the divides between the practices of schools and universities was a difficult yet central part of the facilitation process. The bridging was aided on those occasions in which teachers completed assignments that required them to investigate aspects of their own practice. In this respect teachers collected and examined different types of classroom data, reflected on that data with reference to the broader research literature and considered the implications for their own teaching. Through this research teachers developed both specific classroom strategies for working with their students, and alternative ways of understanding the practices within their classroom and the school. The facilitation needed to encourage teachers to look inwards to their own practice and outwards to the broader research literature and then make connections between the two. While these connections were difficult to create, when they were made, it provided a strong practical purpose for the study that the teachers were undertaking.

Central to facilitation in this context was the development of productive working relationships with and between programme participants. There were some delicate balances to the facilitation process: supporting participants as they investigated aspects of their practice and assessing their assignment work. In any teaching role this is a difficult task, but adding the role of assessor onto the role of supporter was difficult, particularly when having to make judgements about the work completed by colleagues in one school. Likewise, there were balances associated with encouraging school-based collaboration between participants alongside the process of allocating individual marks and grades to assessment tasks.

The level of commitment to study by teachers engaged in this programme was significant as they assumed a new role – a university student engaged in a sustained form of professional learning. Certainly, a key task of facilitation was to sustain this commitment over a long time. Aligned with key ideas on the sustainability of practitioner research partnership in Chapter 4, this seemed to work best when good links could be made between academic research, school classrooms and the teachers' research and writing. Not surprisingly, relationships and communication were crucial here and will be elaborated on in the next chapter. Facilitators in this case needed to balance positive support for teachers as they researched their practice and judgement of their assignment work, which was a culmination of their research.

Case two: facilitating professional learning leadership

This case is based on a three-year partnership between Monash University and the Victorian Department of Education and Early Childhood. The partnership was established as part of a school leadership policy initiative developed by the Department in 2006. As part of this policy a range of partnership programmes were put in place, in which different universities designed programmes for sustained professional learning related to school leadership. The particular partnership reported on in this chapter was called the Leading Professional Learning (LPL) programme that focused on the leadership of professional learning in schools. A cohort of approximately 70 teachers from both primary and secondary schools participated in each year of the programme. The design and delivery of the programme was undertaken by a team of university personnel. The programme was focused on developing and enhancing school-based leadership of professional learning.

The case examines practitioner research and professional learning at two levels: first for the teachers involved in the LPL programme and second for the university team as they reflected on and researched aspects of the programme. Likewise, facilitation existed on two levels. Our goal as university personnel was to facilitate programme participants' learning about the ways in which professional learning could then be facilitated and led in school. The programme process, as well as its content, was strongly underpinned by facilitation strategies and practices that assumed a strong link between practitioner research and professional learning.

The programme had the following components: an initial two-day workshop; a workshop after the first six weeks; a final one-day workshop and online or face-to-face peer support research networks facilitated by a member of the university team. During this time the teachers participating in the programme had to design, evaluate and reflect upon a professional learning project that they implemented in their school.

The initial two-day workshop introduced participants to key ideas related to teacher professional learning, leadership and adult learning. There is considerable research related to these three fields, but relatively little that considers the connections and overlap between them. Indeed it could be argued that the intersection between the three fields represents a form of facilitation (see Figure 5.1).

The university team delivering the programme comprised personnel with expertise in each of these three areas. Through a range of presentations and other small group activities the workshop programme was designed to enable participants to identify the connections between the three areas in ways that related to their own workplace.

A key task for participants to develop as part of the initial workshop was the design of a professional learning project in their school. The professional learning project was established as a form of practitioner research. Participants needed to undertake a series of reconnaissance activities within their school in order to

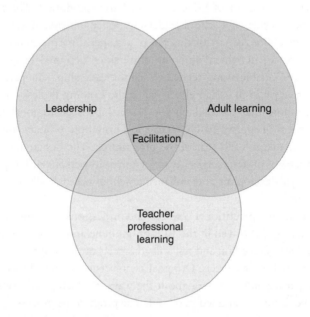

Figure 5.1 Facilitation at the intersection of the leadership, adult learning and professional learning fields.

ascertain school and staff professional learning needs and priorities. The project plan was revised and refined at the mid-session workshop and then implemented over a three- to four-month period. As part of the project participants needed to collect data that would assist project evaluation. The undertaking of the project and associated research was the key vehicle for professional learning.

Following the initial workshop the participants were allocated to peer support research networks comprising ten other participants and one university facilitator. The groups met either in face-to-face settings or through email discussion groups on a semi-regular basis to talk through the implementation of the project. The professional learning projects varied enormously in their scope and focus. Many of the projects sought to encourage school-based practices that supported ongoing teacher inquiry.

To conclude the project the participants attended a final workshop. The focus for this workshop was case writing by the participants. Each participant was asked to write a case based on a dilemma associated with the leadership of their professional learning project. The case writing was the culminating research activity in that it required the participants to critically reflect on their project and prepare that reflection for publication in a book of cases (Berry *et al.*, 2008). The case writing was based on Shulman's (1992) work related to case writing as a means of reflection and professional learning (Loughran, 2008). In Chapter 6 we draw attention to the need to open up the possibilities for more enlightening dialogue between the academy and the field. The writing of cases that were grounded so significantly in practice can be seen to provide an important contribution to our understandings and subsequent knowledge construction regarding such practice.

The case writing proved to be one of the most crucial parts of the facilitation process in the Leading Professional Learning programme. At the final workshop the participants brought in their laptop computers and the goal was to have a good draft of their case complete by the end of the day. The facilitation of the case writing involved an explanation of the background and purposes associated with writing a case; a consideration of some examples of cases; discussion of what could constitute the focus for a case and actual writing of the case over the course of a day. Prompts used to encourage writing and reflection included:

- What is this a case of?
- What are the facts of the case?
- What contextual details are important to help in analysing/understanding the case?
- What issues/tensions/dilemmas do you see in the case?
- What solutions exist/how might you manage the dilemmas?
- What is in the case that would help other identify with it?

- What approach to portrayal would help to strengthen the case and make it engaging for others? (Loughran, 2008)

Following the writing, workshop cases were edited and prepared for publication. The editorial work was conducted by the university team in consultation with the teachers. The purpose in publishing the cases was to record the professional learning from the perspective of the participants, as well as to provide a resource useful for others involved in leading professional learning.

The preparation of the book was a tool useful for bridging the gap between university research and school-based research, as well as for enabling professional learning for both the participating teachers and the university facilitation team. Writing the cases, presenting the cases thematically in books and additional analysis of the cases by members of the university team has provided critical insights pertaining to the processes and practices associated with facilitating teacher inquiry for professional learning (Clemans *et al.*, 2010; Mitchell *et al.*, 2010). In this respect there are two layers of practitioner research and professional learning: the cases are a form of practitioner research revealing the professional learning of the programme participants; the analysis of the cases conducted by the university team is also a form of practitioner research that supported our own professional learning. Both layers of research provide insight into the facilitation of professional learning for those working in schools and universities.

The detail below provides some insights from LPL participants – both teachers and university personnel – regarding the process of facilitation.

In facilitating inquiry through classroom observation in a school one of the teachers provided the following reflection as part of the case writing process.

In order to promote a non-threatening experience for the teacher being observed time was arranged for the two teachers to meet before and after the observation. This provided an opportunity to identify the focus for the observation and for the teacher being observed, the chance to share any peculiarities about the class and to set the scene of the session. The follow-up reflection offered explanation and question time.

It quickly became apparent that these times were invaluable. Professional discourse with a clear focus was evident as both teachers engaged in dialogue. There was no longer one person delivering the learning but rather an exchange of professional learning facilitated through the observation. Age and experience were irrelevant as teachers shared methods, experiences and activities. Strengths and best practice were coming to the fore as well as the realisation that we all 'share' the students . . .

Leading professional learning can be daunting. Leaders can develop the view that they must be all-knowing; yet in reality, it is not the case. Supporting others to identify what they know, what they want to know, what they need to know and where they want to head, and providing opportunities for this to occur just as we do with our students, is what leadership is really all about. I think I have finally embraced and internalised this knowledge.

(case 18, Berry *et al.*, 2008: 57)

The case writing provided this teacher with an opportunity to articulate a set of understandings about facilitating professional learning in terms of practices (such as observation), relationships (based on dialogue) and also in terms of self-under-standing and requisite knowledge. The other cases in the book offer similar reflections on the challenges and successes of facilitating professional learning in a school.

Analysis of the cases sheds some additional light on the facilitation process employed in the LPL programme. In analysing both the process of case writing and the cases themselves, Parr (2008: 12), for example, makes that argument that writing is an important form of professional learning:

Many teachers spoke enthusiastically – and with some considerable surprise – about what they had learned *through the act of writing* and the teacher talk that mediated this writing . . . Teachers, like all researchers if they are honest enough to admit it, do not just *write up* what they have learned. *They write to learn*. They learn through writing.

(emphasis in the original)

The reflection afforded by the writing process was crucial to the means by which participants in the LPL programme investigated their own practice and articulated their key learning. Facilitation of the case writing was therefore critical.

The cases also revealed insights into the relational and emotional experiences of the teachers as they facilitated professional learning in their school (Mitchell, Riley and Loughran, 2010). Some cases reported ways in which the very act of facilitating professional learning was underpinned by strong emotions:

Despite what seemed like a clever plan on my behalf, I was nervous and uncertain about my decision to showcase my leadership skills so soon to my new colleagues. What would happen if I failed? How would my new colleagues view me and how would I feel about myself?

(case 9, Berry *et al.*, 2008: 35)

Others reported ways in which the starting process of facilitation was confronta-tional:

Before my initial presentation to staff, I received the usual jeering:

This better not go too long
What is this all about?
How useful is this going to be?
Do I have to be here?
What am I going to get out of this?

I pressed on knowing I was prepared, my aims were clear and ultimately it
would benefit the teaching and learning at our school.

(case 3, Berry *et al.*, 2008: 21)

Still others reported the productive and rewarding side of such facilitation and
their new found role:

I'm happy to say that after all that initial self-doubt, I'm now a more confident leader of professional learning in my school. I am still learning myself
and I still feel very much part of a team of leaders. I often find myself navigating my learning down an unknown path . . . There may well be sharp
turns and steep declines but I'm more confident now that I'll negotiate a
pathway through it – with the help of my professional learning colleagues.

(case 6, Berry *et al.*, 2008: 29)

In their analysis of cases written by the programme participants, members of the
university team (Clemans *et al.*, 2010) point to ways in which the participants saw
themselves as taking on a new identity as a teacher educator and facilitator of professional learning. The reflections of the participants demonstrated a shift in their
conception of themselves as both teacher and facilitator of professional learning. In
analysing the nature of facilitation, and her own role as a university facilitator in the
LPL programme, Clemans (2008) argues that the identity of the facilitator, who
they are and what they believe, is just as important as the 'what' and 'how' of facilitation. The sense of oneself as being able to guide teacher learning, and promote useful
practitioner research, is based on skill and knowledge, as well as practice and belief.

The LPL programme sought to draw on many of the processes recognised as
useful for facilitating professional learning – a reasonable time frame, establishment of professional community and networks, outside input and school-based
research. What proved to be a crucial part of the facilitation of professional
learning for teachers in this programme was the writing of cases. Furthermore,
the writing conducted by the university team related to the LPP programme and
the cases also constituted a form of professional learning related to the facilitation
processes embedded in all aspects of the LPL programme.

What do the cases say about facilitating professional learning in transformative partnerships?

The cases above have sought to portray some useful and interesting practices associated with facilitating practitioner research for professional learning. In each case there were alignments between the goals and priorities of the participating university and schools. To return to the ideas raised earlier in the chapter, and summarised in Table 5.1, there was an alignment between the institutional meta-practices in both cases – the school and school systems were interested in professional learning partnerships that the universities were able to facilitate. At the meta-practice level there was an assumption that the professional learning would be underpinned by connections between different types of research and the practices in schools and classrooms. These alignments enabled sustained and purposeful institutional partnerships to be established in ways that promoted common sets of 'sayings', 'doings' and 'relatings' concerned with practitioner research and professional learning. Indeed, the formalisation of the partnership arrangements helped to set expectations and provide some structures for the facilitation. These structures helped to establish institutional roles, programme purposes and programme practices. This structuring in part addressed the sort of facilitation tensions that Lendahls Rosendahl and Rönnerman (2006) identified and discussed earlier. While in both cases there were times in which participants' expectations related to the programme purpose and their role diverged and varied, the institutional expectations and structures associated with each programme could be called on to help build common understandings and reinstate roles and responsibilities with the partnerships.

The achievement of substantive and worthwhile professional learning outcomes required careful facilitation. In both cases a key 'saying' espoused by the facilitators was that practitioner research provided a means of achieving professional learning goals. In the first case teachers completed classroom and school-related research projects as part of a programme of study and in order to build their pedagogical knowledge related to the specific needs of students in their classes. In the second case teachers initiated and reflected on a professional learning project in their school in order to build their knowledge and capacity related to school-based leadership of teacher professional learning. Justification of this 'saying' within the two cases was dependent upon the teachers' undertaking or 'doing' practitioner research in their workplace or classroom.

Facilitating the 'doing' of practitioner research in the above two cases aligned with the components of facilitation identified by Poekert (2010) and discussed earlier in the chapter. In each case teachers not only completed class or school-based projects, but also carefully reflected on them through assignment or case writing. In each case there were opportunities for teachers to work both individually and collaboratively. Different forms of scaffolding were employed in each case by the facilitation teams in order to support writing and project work through to completion.

In both of the cases the writing tasks were a key part of the practitioner research process, that is the means of 'relating' research and practice, and therefore the professional learning. Writing assignments, a case or a research paper, provided the means for thoughtful reflection on practice. The process or 'doing' of writing was central to the facilitation of professional learning and constituted a form of research in and of itself (Richardson, 2000). Moreover, the writing provided a means of documenting practice and the ways in which it can be transformed. For teachers in case one this meant identifying teaching and learning strategies useful in their particular school context. For teachers in case two this meant taking on a leadership role in a school and articulating their own leadership skills. For university personnel working in these projects, the act of writing about aspects of the programme helped to explicate some key insights into the processes of professional learning and how that learning could be facilitated. In other words the research provided opportunities to articulate new 'sayings' related to professional learning and teaching practice.

In each case, the 'doing' of the research and writing meant that participants took on new roles. In case one, participants were university students engaging in a programme of study, as well as teachers. In case two, participants were leaders of professional learning in their schools, as well as teachers. The writing tasks were crucial to the nature of professional learning, but also to the participants' sense of role and identity (Clemans, 2008).

The facilitation of professional learning also involved considerable 'bridging' (Rust, 2009) or 'relating' work that made connections between different types of research knowledge, methodologies and different aspects of the professional practice of teachers and university faculty. In both cases teachers accessed research literature related to the professional learning focus. Teachers used research literature to inform their projects and their reflections. In the first case teachers accessed a wide array of research literature related to classroom pedagogy and curriculum. In the second case teachers had access to research related to professional learning, leadership and adult learning. Facilitation involved making this literature meaningful in the practice context.

In each case the 'relatings' between people associated with the facilitation process were crucial to the nature and type of professional learning that took place. This is not surprising, and there is no magic formula that underpins such relationships, but in both cases relationships between participants were built over time, and were most productive when they were underpinned by open exchange and common concern related to the nature of teaching and learning in schools.

The communicative practices and principles associated with such research relationships are developed in the next chapter.

Conclusion

The facilitation in the cases above sought to transform the practices typically associated with teacher professional learning. There were a number of factors that supported the facilitation. Key among these were the individual and institutional commitments made to sustained professional learning over periods of time ranging from six months to three years. In this respect ongoing and formal professional learning was an elemental part of teachers' work. Practitioner research was also fundamental to the facilitation of professional learning in both cases. Various methods of practitioner research provided participants with opportunities to investigate their practice. In both cases the research involved writing as a means of drawing ideas to conclusion, connecting individual practice to other related knowledge and research and explicating new learning.

Facilitation in both cases was a form of pedagogical praxis – it provided the vehicle for enabling particular features of what Ponte and Ax (2011) refer to as the 'what', 'how' and 'why' of practitioner research as a worthwhile form of professional learning. Facilitation required knowledge of professional learning, of practitioner research and of different aspects of teachers' work in schools and classrooms. Facilitation required building relationships and 'bridging' the institutional cultures and practices of school and universities so that knowledge and ideas could be exchanged. Facilitation also required providing a rationale for practitioner research as a tool that enables worthwhile and sustained professional learning linked to practice. In the two cases above, such a rationale helped participants not only deepen their understanding of their professional practice, but also augment their sense of 'who' they are as researchers and teachers in their schools.

References

Berry, A., Blaise, M., Loughran, J., Mitchell, J., Parr, G. and Robb, D. (Eds) (2008). *Leading professional learning: Cases of professional dilemmas.* Melbourne: Victoria Department of Education and Early Childhood Development and Monash University.

Carr, W. and Kemmis, S. (1986). *Becoming critical: Education, knowledge and action research.* Victoria, Australia: Deakin University.

Clemans, A. (2008). Who counts just as much as what and how. In A. Berry, M. Blaise, A. Clemans, J. Loughran, J. Mitchell, G. Parr, P. Riley and D. Robb (Eds) *Leading professional learning: Cases of professional dilemmas* (pp. 187–188). Melbourne: Victoria Department of Education and Early Childhood Development and Monash University.

Clemans, A., Berry, A. and Loughran, J. (2010). Lost and found in transition: The professional journey of teacher educators. *Professional Development in Education*, 36(1–2): 211–228.

Cochran-Smith, M. and Demers, K. (2010). Research and teacher learning: Taking an inquiry stance. In O. Kwo (Ed.) *Teachers as learners: Critical discourses on challenges and opportunities* (pp. 13–44). Hong Kong: Springer.

Erickson, G., Minnes-Brandes, G., Mitchell, I. and Mitchell, J. (2005). Collaborative teacher learning: Findings from two professional development projects. *Teaching and Teacher Education*, 21(7): 787–798.

Furlong, J. (2005). Afterword (for theme edition: Professional Learning for Teachers in Australia). *Journal of In-service Education*, 31(4): 747–750.

Groundwater-Smith, S. and Mockler, N. (2009). *Teacher professional learning in an age of compliance: Mind the gap.* Dordrecht: Springer.

Grundy, S. and Robinson, J. (2004). Teacher professional development: Themes and trends in the recent Australian experience. In C. Day and J. Sachs (Eds) *International handbook on the continuing professional development of teachers* (pp. 146–166). Maidenhead, Berkshire: Open University Press.

Hoban, G.F. (2002). *Teacher learning for educational change.* Buckingham and Philadelphia: Open University Press.

Kemmis, S. (2009). Action research as a practice-based practice. *Educational Action Research*, 17(3): 463–474.

Kemmis, S. and Grootenboer, P. (2008). Situating praxis in practice: Practice architectures and the cultural, social and material conditions for practice. In S Kemmis and T. Smith (Eds) *Enabling practice. Challenges for education* (pp. 37–62). Rotterdam/Taipei: Sense Publishers.

Kemmis, S. and Smith, T. (2008). Praxis and praxis development. In S. Kemmis and T. Smith (Eds) *Enabling praxis* (pp. 3–13). Rotterdam: Sense Publishers.

Lehndahls Rosendahl, B. and Rönnerman, K. (2006). Facilitating school improvement: The problematic relationship between researchers and practitioners. *Journal of In-service Education*, 32(4): 497–509.

Loughran, J. (2003). Exploring the nature of teacher research. In A. Clarke and G. Erickson (Eds) *Teacher inquiry: Living the research in everyday practice* (pp. 181–189). London and New York: RoutledgeFalmer.

Loughran, J. (2008). Recognising the knowledge of practice through cases. In A. Berry, M. Blaise, A. Clemans, J. Loughran, J. Mitchell, G. Parr and D. Robb (Eds) *Leading professional learning: Cases of professional dilemmas* (pp. 3–7). Melbourne: Victoria Department of Education and Early Childhood Development and Monash University.

Mitchell, I. (2007). Professional learning: Moving from professional talk to teacher research. In A. Berry, A. Clemans and A. Kostogriz (Eds) *Dimensions of professional learning: Professionalism, practice and identity* (pp. 105–119). Rotterdam: Sense Publishers.

Mitchell, J., Hayes, D. and Mills, M. (2010). Crossing school and university boundaries to reshape professional learning and research practices. *Professional Development in Education*, 36(3): 491–509.

Mitchell, J., Riley, P. and Loughran, J. (2010). Leading professional learning in schools: Emotion in action. *Teacher Development, 14*(4): 533–547.

Mockler, N. (2005). Trans/forming teachers: New professional learning and transformative teacher professionalism. *Journal of In-service Education, 31*(4): 733–746.

Parr, G. (2008). Writing about learning: Learning through writing. In A. Berry, M. Blaise, A. Clemans, J. Loughran, J. Mitchell, G. Parr, P. Riley and D. Robb (Eds) *Leading professional learning: Cases of professional dilemmas* (pp. 9–12). Melbourne: Victoria Department of Education and Early Childhood Development and Monash University.

Poekert, P. (2010). The pedagogy of facilitation: Teacher inquiry as professional development in a Florida elementary school. *Professional Development in Education, 37*(1): 19–38.

Ponte, P. and Ax, J. (2011). Inquiry-based professional learning in educational praxis: Knowing why, what and how. In N. Mockler and J. Sachs (Eds) *Rethinking educational practice through reflexive inquiry: Essays in honour of Susan Groundwater-Smith* (pp. 49–60). Dordrecht: Springer.

Richardson, L. (2000). Writing: A method of inquiry. In N. Denzin and Y. Lincoln (Eds) *Handbook of qualitative research* (2nd edition) (pp. 923–946). Thousand Oaks: Sage Publications Inc.

Rönnerman, K. (2005). Participant knowledge and the meeting of practitioners and researchers. *Pedagogy, Culture and Society, 13*(3): 291–311.

Rust, F. (2009). Teacher research and the problem of practice. *Teachers College Record, 111*(8): 1882–1893.

Schön, D. (1987). *Educating the reflective practitioner: Toward a new design for teaching and learning in the professions.* San Francisco: Jossey-Bass.

Schön, D.A. (1991). *The reflective turn: Case studies in and on educational practice.* New York: Teachers College Press.

Shulman, J. (1992). *Case methods in teacher education.* New York: Teachers College Press.

Webster-Wright, A. (2009). Reframing professional development through understanding authentic professional learning. *Review of Educational Research, 79*(2): 702–739.

Chapter 6

Communicability

Susan Groundwater-Smith, the lead author of this chapter, originally convened the Coalition of Knowledge Building Schools that forms the case around which this chapter is built. Almost from the beginning, Nicole Mockler has also played a significant role in the development and maintenance of the Coalition. As the chapter demonstrates, the alliance has some specific characteristics that make it a suitable subject for discussing the ways in which the academy and schools can communicate with each other in ways that enhance practice. It draws out the conditions that are required for each party to have an authentic voice and reveals that each contributes to professional knowledge production.

Introduction

Communicability, that is the capacity of all parties to speak with and understand each other, is never unproblematic; particularly when it is the case that two different worlds, the world of academia and the world of practice, may be in danger of colliding. If facilitation in partnerships is to be effective and go beyond its capacity to be transactional; if it is to have a real purchase in the sphere of the academic and on the field of practice then those engaged in the act of investigating and making sense of practice must be able to speak and to listen, to hear and to understand, to challenge and debate. The communicative milieu must not only restrict itself to the kind of engagement that is purely functional but must move to one that opens up new possibilities for dialogue and change.

It has been argued by Dressman (2008) that much of the language of contemporary social theory, as employed by academics, is both impenetrable and of little use to practitioners who may wish to adopt ideas and concepts that have the potential to liberate them from previously held cherished beliefs. He likens such language to a complex Gordian Knot. However, while the original knot sliced in half by Alexander was of one thread, the discourses of social theory are 'composed of multiple, interwoven and quite frequently discontinuous threads wound sometimes round themselves and sometimes around multiple branching axes with no single centre' (ibid.: 15). Much contemporary social theory used by academics sees the world as 'contingent, ungrounded, diverse, unstable, indeterminate, a set of disunified cultures or interpretations, which breed a degree of scepticism about the objectivity of truth, history and norms, the givenness of natures and the coherence of identities' (Eagleton, 1996: vii). Such contradictory and pluralist thinking can lead to confusion and uncertainty. Not always a bad thing, but when one is intent upon informed action then the language of practice requires clarity and direction.

We are wary of producing a melange of possibilities that can paralyse those with an interest in social affairs and the possibility of change. We certainly see a need for a more nuanced understanding that will fight and resist false dichotomies and this requires well-developed and sophisticated arguments that can be so articulated that they are open to challenge and question; but, that such arguments are also warranted and defendable. If one cannot fully understand and engage with what is being proposed then it means that the footings are slippery, to say the least. By expecting that speakers, within the context of shared inquiry, will reveal their reasoning and the basis for their argument in terms that can be clearly apprehended by the listeners, then those listeners will be enabled to apply criteria that can allow them to determine whether statements are, to the best of their knowledge, true or untrue, right or wrong, appropriate or inappropriate. Thus dissonant views may be expressed and themselves tested and the emerging professional knowledge reconstituted and action reconsidered. Furthermore, as we shall argue later in this chapter, it is not sufficient for such debate to only be conducted at the local level, but that it should also be one that can be engaged in widely through publication in traditional channels as well as new media.

Thus, the key issues for this chapter are the following.

- While transactional facilitation requires communication that will enable the smooth functioning of practitioner research, transformational facilitation is built upon a reciprocal recognition of the capacities of each party and is enabled by significant dialogue.
- Communication goes beyond discussions internal to any one project, important as that is, and is employed to develop and disseminate ideas to the educational world, locally, regionally and globally; so that making practitioner research available for authentic critique means publishing beyond the immediate project and developing a form of participation that enables a variety of media to be employed to disseminate what has been undertaken as well as what has been learned.
- Forms of engagement, as has been argued in previous chapters, are inclusive and interconnected.

In order to make these issues concrete we have chosen to offer here an extended example that will act to scaffold the case for communicability that is transformational and that is revealing of the many challenges and opportunities available to those who choose to work in the manner outlined in this book.

Placing this chapter in context

Throughout this work we have contrasted facilitation that is transactional with a strong instrumental functional focus and that which is transformational with its press to the emancipatory. We have expressed an ongoing concern for attention to be paid to education as praxis and among a number of definitions we include that of Kemmis and Smith (2008: 16), with praxis being:

> Purposive action, right educational conduct which is guided by moral purpose greater than the purpose of producing learning. Teaching which aims at no more than producing some particular piece of learning is not educational praxis.

The case that will inform this chapter is the formation and practice of the Coalition of Knowledge Building Schools (Black-Hawkins, 2008; Mockler and Groundwater-Smith, 2011; Needham, 2011). The Coalition has been functioning in New South Wales for over 10 years and currently has 13 schools among its members. It is a hybrid collection of schools in that a number are located in Metropolitan Sydney while others are located in regional NSW. Many are facing very difficult circumstances but some cater for students from relatively privileged backgrounds. There are both coeducational schools and single sex schools, primary schools and secondary schools and the group includes a school that provides short-term respite care for young people whose home lives are disrupted by illness or forms of domestic violence. As well, the Coalition has a group of related organisations with which it works ranging from the Australian Museum through to the State Library and the Zoo Education Centre. Members have in common a desire to systematically investigate practice, employ student voice and work with university partners on an equal footing. The Coalition's website (www. ckbs.org) includes further information about member schools, academic partners and 'friends' of the Coalition.

The work of the Coalition can be seen as a case that can exemplify the formation of transformative partnerships, to be compared with what Wenger (1998: 126) has referred to as a 'constellation of practice' in that the various participating organisations are distinctive, but interrelated with shared fundamental values and a desire to inform one another and the wider community of their various instances of practitioner inquiry. As Wenger puts it, 'the term *constellation* refers to a group of stellar objects that are seen as a configuration even though they may not be particularly close to one another, of the same kind, or of the same size' (p. 127). The alliance meets Wenger's requirements in a number of ways, such as having related enterprises, sharing artefacts, having geographical relations, intentionally straddling boundaries so that members can speak to each other of their enterprises and reinterpret each other's way of addressing and solving educational challenges. In effect the Coalition is opening up what Kemmis (2011: 16–18) refers to as the 'communicative space' wherein those participating strive both subjectively and intersubjectively to reach shared understandings of practice by understanding how that practice has evolved over time by identifying issues that arise out of their shared *lifeworlds* and administrative and economic *systems* as discussed in the first chapter of this book.

We shall pay particular attention to the ways in which the consequential stakeholders in the educational enterprise, namely the school students, are also a part of the communicative process.

Before proceeding to discuss the exemplary case and its ramifications for the ways in which professional dialogue that is mutually constitutive and respectful can be conducted, it is important to first understand something of the nature of school education in Australia, in a general sense, and Sydney in New South Wales in particular. This history has been responsible for often impeding communication, not only between the fields of practice and academia, but also within the field itself. Until recently the six Australian States and two territories have carried the major responsibility for education while the Federal Government, with its taxing powers, determines funding for schools. However, current initiatives have resulted in an ambition by the Commonwealth to work towards: a national curriculum; tests and reporting on student performance; workforce reform through the harmonisation of teacher registration, recruitment and retention policies and the reduction of red tape across the various employing authorities particularly with regard to the health and safety of students. While this commitment to collaborative federalism is a strong ambition of the national government, it is not one that has been easily achieved and continues to be contested both by government school systems within States and Territories and by the non-government sector.

Most troubling among the issues is the matter of school funding. The school mix in Australia is a complex one. The proportion of Australian students attending non-government schools has risen steadily over the past three decades from 21 per cent of students in 1977 to 34 per cent of students in 2007 (Australian National Audit Office, 2008–2009). Whereas some 66 per cent of young people attend government schools that are secular in nature the remainder are enrolled in Catholic systemic schools[1] and 'Independent Schools'; the latter providing for some 14 per cent of students, with most being high status, high fee-paying schools many of which are faith-based. This is significant for the Coalition in that its members come from all of these sectors. This would normally result in combative relationships fed by the industrial climate and often also by the media. Among the many complex issues in this matter of funding is the view that support for wealthy schools is inequitable and unfair (Campbell and Sherington, 2006). This has led to a number of acrimonious disputes between the sectors. Of course, as Wilkinson, Caldwell, Selleck, Harris and Dettman (2007: 8) have observed:

> The state aid debate is not unique to Australia. The matter of state or public funding for non-government or private schools has been vigorously contested in other countries. The outcomes have been varied, ranging from the Netherlands, where it is unconstitutional and therefore illegal to distinguish between public and private schools in the allocation of public funds, to the United States, where it is unconstitutional and therefore illegal to provide any funding to private schools that have a connection to a church. In some countries the matter was settled decades ago, and it is not now the lively field of debate as it is in Australia.

While all major political parties support state aid it is resolutely opposed by the various teachers' unions and a number of parent groups. It is argued that the drift from the government school sector has led to a residualisation effect whereby, in many communities, the state school is the resort of last choice (Dowling, 2007). Thus generative and collaborative dialogue between schools in the Coalition is the exception rather than the rule.

Under normal conditions it would be unlikely that such a hybrid group of schools catering for very different student bodies would find themselves in partnership with each other and with academics from two different universities (one metropolitan, one regional) and with a consultant leading a coaching and mentoring organization and, finally, representatives of Sydney's leading Museum, the Zoo Education Facility and the State Library. Furthermore, it is not only the professionals from these very different sites who meet with one another on a regular basis, but their students, from time to time, participate in enterprises where they come together to contribute to a range of challenging activities. Thus this case is noteworthy for contributing to our understanding of communicability and how it might function where we are seeking to establish a transformational relationship.

The evolution of the Coalition of Knowledge Building Schools

How then has The Coalition of Knowledge Building Schools (CKBS) group been welded and knitted together as the aforementioned constellation of practice? Mockler and Groundwater-Smith (2011: 295) have likened the process to the construction of a spider's web.

> In seeking for a metaphor for the establishment of the Coalition of Knowledge Building Schools, the manufacture of a web most closely approximates the ways in which the community has been established . . . In our account of the history of the Coalition . . . it is clear that there was a number of steps analogous to the work of the spider. Initially a modest bridge was built between a small number of participating schools. The Centre for Practitioner Research (CPR)[2] in the Faculty of Education and Social Work provided a hub and frame that would enable the web to be built and strengthened. The 'stickiness' of the threads paralleled the agreed principles by which the Coalition would function.

The aforementioned Centre for Practitioner Research was established in 1998, following the given metropolitan university's successful hosting of the Inaugural International Practitioner Research Conference.[3] It has always been unfunded and has been seen to be part of the remit of one of the authors of this book in her role as Honorary Professor. Within the Faculty of Education and Social Work it sits within the Division of Professional Learning associated with that Division's service to the community.

The two aims of the CPR were set down as:

1   To validate and value the research-based knowledge created by practitioners in the field.
2   To develop cross-disciplinary networks to facilitate the production and circulation of new knowledge.

Its purposes were seen to be:

- to foster, support and enhance practitioner research as a mode of inquiry to understand and improve practice in universities and schools locally, nationally and internationally;
- to contribute to the creation of situated knowledge regarding educational practices;
- to investigate and critique the outcomes of practitioner research;
- to encourage the development, validation and documentation of new methodologies in practitioner research;
- to act as a forum for the discussion of practitioner research via conferences, electronic and print media;
- to establish international affiliations with universities and schools similarly engaged.

Its range of activities included conducting free-to-the-public 'twilight seminars', developing professional practice links with networked learning communities in the UK and mainland Europe and reaching out to other sites for learning beyond the classroom, such as the Australian Museum, and building and nurturing a networked professional learning community. Thus it may be seen that the CKBS has its roots in the concept of a faculty of education having a responsibility to contribute to professional practice employing a range and variety of media. As Sachs (2011: 156), who was a foundation member of the CPR, has noted, models for informing teacher professional learning have had as their purpose retooling, remodelling, revitalising and reimagining. In the case of the latter she sees educators having the courage to ask tough questions and seek for honest answers. The CPR had the capacity to lay down those conditions for critical dialogue between the academy and the field.

It was arising from the initial work of the CPR that a small number of schools were identified who clearly had an interest in engaging in systematic inquiry. Following some early meetings they came together to form the nucleus of the Coalition. By 2002 seven schools (three independent and four government) had gathered together to more formally outline their shared purposes, these being:

- to develop and enhance the notion of evidence-based practice;[4]
- to develop an interactive community of practice using appropriate technologies;
- to make a contribution to a broader professional knowledge base with respect to educational practice;
- to build research capability within their own and each other's schools by engaging both teachers and students in the research processes; and
- to share methodologies which are appropriate to practitioner inquiry as a means of transforming teacher professional learning.

(Groundwater-Smith and Mockler, 2003: 1)

The coalition at work

In order to demonstrate the dialogic and reciprocal work of the CKBS, as it has grown over the decade, four brief narratives of practice have been selected, paying attention to the ways in which the partnerships between participating schools and academic practitioners have been played out and how the various stakeholders, in their interactions and productions, have escaped the traps of those often obscure discursive formations so beloved of the academy.

Narrative 1 – beating the bullies

Over a span of two years a comprehensive girls high school, once a member of the Coalition, undertook an investigation regarding bullying among girls and its consequences for the emotional well-being of young people. A noteworthy feature of the work was the formation of a student advisory committee that would both inform and drive the inquiry. Among the many strategies that were adopted was one whereby students who had experienced bullying over a period of time were able to record their experiences. Each student was asked to select a name for herself and the purpose of the interview was explained. Each student gave her informed consent. At the conclusion to the interview each girl was asked to 'give a message to your teachers'. One such story is reproduced below.

April is in Year 9. She began the interview by emphasising that it was her desire to help, not only herself but others who were experiencing being bullied. Her story revolves around a specific, difficult and ongoing relationship. Her adversary often sends her SMS messages. She seems to go out of her way to alienate April's friends. At one point she had a more positive relationship with April and this makes it even more difficult because she is in a position to disclose confidences.

April's parents have counselled her to give the bullying student 'time and things will settle down'; but she doesn't believe that they will. 'It is all very hurtful.' As a way of 'chilling out' April uses her local youth group who are not involved in the school. She believes that she has to be active in focusing on 'school stuff, learning to prioritise what matters'. She has discovered that crying is not a solution; if anything, if she is seen to be crying or have been crying, it makes matters worse.

She sees that some students just seem to be 'targets' but can't explain why this is so. Without using the phrase, she described a clear social 'pecking order' where those at the bottom of the heap are continuously 'picked on'. It means that students have to be able to read the order. 'If you hang out with people lower down, you are picked on too – you're a loser.' She is puzzled about how she can get into other students' 'good books and feel wanted' especially because she doesn't want to conform to the mores of a group that 'smoke and play cool'.

The class dynamics play quite a part in what takes place. April gave the example of what happened when a new girl arrived and for a short time she felt quite accepted.

She has experienced some physical encounters, including face slapping. Threats have included 'I'm going to kill you'. While she doesn't believe them, they are unnerving nonetheless.

When she first started at High School April thought she could handle things herself. But she found that she was ineffectual. She went to the counsellor who provided some support, but when she approached her Year Advisor she was told 'Just ignore it'. In the end her parents intervened. She strongly feels that if the Year Advisor is not able to handle the problem then that person should not have that role. The Year Advisor and students 'must be able to talk to each other and have confidence in each other'.

April was very adamant that she wanted her teachers to hear her message:

> You don't understand what it is like to be a teenager today. We're growing up faster, there's a lot of early maturing. Boys are always being discussed. You have to dress cool and smoke. If students say they are being bullied, believe them otherwise they feel worse still. But don't address it straight away in class or they'll (the bullies) go for their victim when the class is finished. It's not a laughing matter, it's not trivial, students need someone to believe them, someone to talk to.

April concluded by saying 'This wasn't the easiest thing I've ever done!'

Student stories such as this were used to investigate with staff the ways in which the anecdotes challenged their professional values and beliefs about bullying and its consequences. They were asked to consider how they might have formulated these beliefs, how they saw themselves dealing ethically with the situation and how the school's current strategies and policies might change.

The work in this project is notable for several reasons. The school Principal and the academic 'critical friend' worked closely with both the student advisory committee and staff members to ensure that the project would have maximum impact on not only the school itself, but also more broadly. They went on to publish accounts of the work at two international conferences (Needham and Groundwater-Smith, 2003; Needham, 2005). It is also interesting to note that with a later change of Principal the commitment of the school to the Coalition waned, but the outgoing Principal continues to make an important contribution to the Coalition as an independent consultant in coaching and mentoring school leaders.

Narrative 2 – a methodological debate

This was a study of a complex formative evaluation of a comprehensive Year 9 innovation in one of the large independent girls' schools that are currently members of the Coalition. The project was known as The Year 9 Laboratory and was seen by the school to be an innovation within the ambit of continuous school reform in what might be seen as an 'activist' school. It is not the intention, here, to outline the project itself other than to note that it was one that focused on student independence, engagement and resilience. A wide range of both quantitative and qualitative procedures was employed in the evaluation and their complementarities considered within a discussion of the utilisation of mixed methods in a single case. The study itself was presented at the annual conference of the Australian Association for Research in Education (Groundwater-Smith, Martin, Hayes, Herrett, Layhe, Layman and Saurine, 2006).

The research team comprised both insider and external researchers. The external team included an academic practitioner, functioning as a critical friend and who would examine student and teacher perceptions of ongoing developments using focus group inquiry, observation and shadowing and would act as the research co-ordinator, and an educational psychologist who would explore the psychological impacts using motivation and engagement measures. The insider team was comprised of the Head of Senior School, the Director of Studies, the Coordinator of the Year 9 programme and a Year 9 mentor and science teacher. The in-house team monitored the ongoing findings of the external group and engaged in their own inquiry, 'Making Learning Visible', that mapped student achievement in Year 9 mediated by a series of individual student interviews in which they discussed their orientation to and enjoyment of learning. Supporting the inquiry was a student advisory group and a parent reference group. The interaction between the teams, their various perspectives and expertise and the methods that they employed enabled the emergence of a rich and innovative research design.

The inclusion of this narrative demonstrates the ways in which academic partners and school-based practitioners can work together, over a period of time, to not only examine the results of the formative evaluation but also to analyse the ways in which various inquiry methods contribute to our understandings of practice thus demonstrating one of the essential tenets of the Coalition: to 'develop and enhance the notion of evidence based practice'. As Biesta (2011: 181) has noted, the idea of some kind of unsullied 'research paradigm' is typically Anglo-American and that in the continental traditions there is a much stronger emphasis upon the kind of explanation and understanding that can emanate from a mixed methods approach such as the one adopted here. (See also Chapter 2.)

Narrative 3 – birds of paradise

From time to time the Australian Museum's audience research unit draws upon the Coalition for advice from young people regarding their exhibition plans. The unit regularly consult groups of students whose schools participate in the Coalition of Knowledge Building Schools. The attraction of the Coalition is that it is, as has already been observed, a hybrid community of practice composed of schools from a range of socio-economic regions, rural and metropolitan. These day-long meetings involve students from a range of different Coalition schools and have been well documented (Kelly and Groundwater-Smith, 2009). Most recently the Museum called upon students to examine its proposals for a new temporary exhibition featuring Birds of Paradise and to subsequently visit the exhibition and evaluate it.

For the purposes of this exercise two schools were approached. One was an independent girls' school, the other a metropolitan boys' school with students whose backgrounds were mainly Middle Eastern and Pacific Islander. Altogether 19 students attended the workshop. Their respective schools were visited prior to the event and teachers were briefed on the design of the day and images of Birds of Paradise were made available. In the case of the boys' school it was also possible to speak briefly with the boys themselves. These processes were used to provide advance organisers for the students who were asked to reflect upon something 'amazing' that they had experienced – the rationale being that the birds themselves were exotic and arresting in their appearance.

The Head of Audience Research explained that exhibitions took anything from six months to two years to plan. Teams were made up of a range of people functioning in different roles. Many of the Birds of Paradise team were going to be present during the day to hear what students had to say. She pointed out that in the past audience research was seen as an evaluative function at the end of an exhibition, but that now the focus was far more on collecting information prior to the mounting of the exhibition itself. Furthermore, students were given the opportunity to 'go behind the scenes' and see how the bird collection was processed and stored.

During subsequent discussions students had a number of questions and observations, such as how the headdresses were kept on, *how* the birds were collected (did the birds have to die, or were they already dead?). They noticed that all the materials worn were natural and crafted; they wondered about when the ceremonial dress would be worn on what kinds of special occasions. Some students with a Pacific Island background compared what they had seen to their own conventions, such as it is the women who wear feathers but in Papua and New Guinea this decoration was limited to men. They saw the dancing as mirroring that of the birds and wondered about why that would be so; were the male dancers also hoping to impress the females?

The student commentary focused on the proposed text for the exhibition and the design of the interactives. They noted that little attention had been paid to the needs of the non-English speaking backgrounds of some visitors and that more planning was required to address matters of cultural sensitivity. They also developed a plethora of ideas for promoting the exhibition and developing eye-catching slogans.

They felt comfortable in delivering their key messages, some of which were quite critical of the intended exhibition; at the same time they applauded the Museum's willingness to listen to them and respect them.

The pattern here was of inclusive and interactive dialogue representative of many encounters of this kind between young people and professional practitioners from schools, the university and the Australian Museum itself. All were able to join in the conversation about what was to be done and the range of perspectives and experience was respected. Importantly, the museum, in its desire to share this work has created a blogspot (http://australianmuseum.net.au/blogpost/Audience-Research-Blog/How-would-you-design-an-exhibit-Meeting-Part-1), one of many that outlines partnership work with the Coalition drawing increasingly on new media.

While space does not permit a full explanation of the follow-up meeting, it is important to note that the Museum saw that it had a responsibility to demonstrate to the students the ways in which their suggestions had been taken into account. In the earlier discussion students had expressed concern regarding the display of 'skins'; these are unmounted birds, where the intention of display is to demonstrate subtle differences between female birds who do not have the exotic plumage of the males. As a means of avoiding confronting museum visitors with a showcase of bird carcases that the students found so emotionally disengaging, the skins were placed under misty glass that only clarified as one looked directly down through it. The students were delighted by the solution and indicated to the Museum their pleasure that their concerns had been noted and had informed part of the display.

Fielding and Moss (2011: 79) write of the need for 'restless encounters' that allow for radically different relationships to be formed between those who normally hold sway. They write of this in the context of schools, but the concept equally applies to these out-of-school institutional setting where normally the Museum would hold its visitors at arms length. Fielding and Moss argue that such encounters allow participants to

> [R]e-see each other as persons rather than as role occupants, and in so doing nurture not only a new understanding, sense of possibility and felt respect between adults and young people, but also a joy in each other's being and a greater sense of delight and responsibility.
>
> (ibid.: 79)

Narrative 4 – can we influence change?

In brief, this project was designed to enable school students from a significantly disadvantaged boys' high school, as a member of the Coalition, to act as 'clients' advising architecture students of their beliefs and desires regarding their school environment. Its reciprocal purpose was to bring to architecture students an authentic challenge whereby they would be engaged in a form of respectful inquiry that would enable them to learn about design that supports social and environmental sustainability.

Young people in schools are rarely consulted about the nature of the environment in which they function, even at a time when there is an increasing understanding that there needs to be a transformation of school environs as an essential component of re-imagining education in the twenty-first century. As Burke (2007: 363) has observed, children and young people are steeped in a 'visual cultural world from their earliest years through to adolescence [but] may be considered to be a poorly understood and under-used resource in envisaging the possibilities of the school of the future'.

While this project was limited to the outdoor areas of the school it provided us with evidence that when the young people are taken seriously they can make a significant contribution to issues related to design and architecture. The project was seen by the school as one that would engage the senior boys as active citizens who might have a voice in considering their outdoor environment and whose views and preferences in all of their diversity *would* be respected and honoured. As Lawson (2001) has observed, if citizenship education is to nurture a sense of belonging in the community and connection to the school, then it needs to address issues of diversity and identity. This is of particular consequence for students from this setting.

In many ways this was a problematic project in that it crossed a number of different boundaries and disciplines (Beale, 2008). It required careful steering to account for not only the framing of the school students, but also the university students, academic staff and partners and school leaders. Progressive and transformative learning environments will only emerge out of authentically reciprocal partnerships between the various actors. This ability to take a proactive role in such undertakings grows out of experiences such as this collaboration that took the exploration to those for whom the design would most matter; the young people themselves.

The academic partners from Architecture and Design and from Education presented together a discussion of the ways in which two disciplinary fields can benefit from border crossing both literally and figuratively while at the same time engaging young people as 'clients' and treating them seriously (Groundwater-Smith and Rubbo, 2010). Thus this fourth narrative of practice demonstrates a form of lateral communication between university faculties with different traditions and practices as well as managing the communicative challenges of mediating interactions between high-achieving university students and boys, most of whom had little or no experience of what a university might be and how they might aspire to enter one.

Narratives of practice and the communicative space

It is not intended that these four narratives of practice arising from the work of the CKBS should be taken as merely celebratory. It is argued that they provide evidence of the ways in which the complex and overlapping relationships between the key players went beyond the kind of transactional facilitation that would enable the smooth functioning of the projects and moved towards the transformational in that significant change was enabled.

There is no template for establishing and sustaining an alliance such as the Coalition. However, there are communicative features that it embraces that have been documented by Needham (2011) as one who has participated in its work over a significant period of time. Following a set of processes built upon those of appreciative inquiry (Cooperrider, Whitney and Stavros, 2008), she sought to 'distil aspects of the network's function in relation to professional learning' (p. 264) as well as school development that was assisted by transformational facilitation. She identified, in particular, the ways in which meetings and day-long conferences were conducted, describing them as informal, open, friendly and sharing, taking on a collective responsibility for action. The meetings were not an end in themselves, but acted as the ongoing social glue that held the group together with individual member organisations taking from them a sense of shared substantive moral purpose and an ability to look beyond the immediate environment with its challenges and constraints. As one respondent reported:

> The Coalition has been a source of inspiration to me in my practice. Despite the differences in school contexts there has always been something to take away. We work in 'confined spaces' ours being the world of low SES communities (high rates of illiteracy and low numeracy, dysfunctional families and poor social skills) with a high need for equity funding, and sometimes we do not have opportunities to see outside.
>
> (Needham, 2011: 209)

Thus in each of the projects reported above the communicative space was inhabited by a range of participants, and the subsequent professional knowledge that was generated was mediated by the sociocultural, material and technical arrangements available in each of the sites. Returning to Schatzki (2002, 2005) whose work was discussed in the opening chapter to this book, practices are not only to be understood cognitively, but they also have an affective and embodied dimension. We cannot consign to each project a set of routines that will provide a template for others, but rather we need to understand them as being generated and located within the respective social sites that both enable and constrain. Similarly, Wenger (1998: 47), who also acts as a touchstone to our theorising about transformational partnerships as constellations of practice, argues that 'practice connotes doing, but not just doing in and of itself. It is doing in an historical and social context that gives structure and meaning to what we do. In this sense practice is always social'.

At the same time, the practices of those participating in these four narratives are not exclusively confined to the particular sites. As Needham (2011) claims, the strength of the Coalition is that practices and initiatives are shared and discussed, and can facilitate the generation of collective professional knowledge across sites. In effect the Coalition becomes a collector with various ideas coupled and interwoven to form new ways of thinking. That the Coalition lives up to its name of being a professional knowledge building organisation is not only demonstrable in the range and variety of publications that it has spawned, some of which have been cited above, but also in the ways in which its members take initiatives to interact with each other and offer advice and insight. Currently two members, both of whom are in receipt of Australian National Partnership Funding designed to assist schools in low SES communities, are working together to develop protocols for students from each school to observe teaching practices in the other. Youth participation in teacher education, for that is what is intended here, is a particularly delicate and fragile course for member schools to take. Mitchell, Weber and Yoshida (2008) have argued for more attention to be paid to conversations around teacher professional learning that includes the young people themselves – mobilising young people as activists is clearly a part of this professional knowledge building enterprise.

Summary and conclusion

In this chapter we have been mindful of the various communicative media that might be employed to share and critically discuss practice. For all parties to join in the communicative space it is necessary that those for whom academic discourse is unfamiliar should be supported in being able to portray their practices using their own authentic voice. By referencing the case of the Coalition we have provided evidence of field-based practitioners and academic partners working together, writing together and presenting at conferences. We have discussed the pitfalls of employing overly convoluted and inaccessible language and argued for a discourse that recognises complexity but does not mask it such that it is no longer understandable.

We have seen the merits of a two-way conversational track and made a case for professional knowledge to be made available to the profession through a variety of means, over and above academic journals with their limited readership. We also recognise the power and potential of the new social media where both academics and field-based practitioners have to learn to make their way together.

What we are concerned with here is the authentic sharing and construction of occupational practice. Fielding *et al.* (2005: 101) quote Posch on the nature of 'dynamic networks' that best equates with the practices of the Coalition. Posch suggests that such networks can be contrasted with hierarchical networks that are managed from above. Dynamic networks are characterised by symmetry, a capacity for exchange, shared interests and are multidimensional. They quote Posch in summing up dynamic networks when he argues that 'the essential feature is the autonomous and flexible establishment of relationships to assist responsible action in the face of complexity and uncertainty' (Fielding *et al.*, 2005: 101).

Finally, we have attended to the words of Fals Borda (2000: 633) when he advocated:

> The need to practice in such a way that it gives a moral and humanistic orientation to the work of the activist researcher; and, to gain a sense of personal commitment that combines the logic of action and the logic of research.

He argued that the duty of the participatory action researcher was not just to identify and analyse the social reality of the conditions under which people live but to be active in remedying those conditions. In this chapter we have opened up the possibility that the participatory action researcher can also include, in the context of education, the consequential stakeholders themselves. With goodwill, generosity and openness the communicative space can be expanded such that our schools can become satisfying and optimistic sites of practice.

Notes

1   In addition, there is a small number of Anglican, Lutheran and Seventh Day Adventist systemic schools.
2   Re-named the Practitioner Research Special Interest Group (PR SIG) in 2006 in accordance with University policies regarding the naming and functioning of centres.
3   This conference built upon a series held at the Institute of Education, Cambridge.
4   This term is one that the Coalition has embraced in its broadest sense, seeking to problematise its current usage and redefine it to mean evidence that is gathered in a forensic rather than adversarial sense. For further discussion see Groundwater-Smith and Mockler (2002).

References

Australian National Audit Office (2008–2009). *ANAO Audit Report #45: Funding for non-government schools.* http://www.anao.gov.au/uploads/documents/2008-09_Audit_Report_45.pdf Accessed 1 February, 2011.

Beale, N. (2008). Young people, citizenship, health and participatory research. *ACME Editorial Collective and International E-Journal for Critical Geographies, 7*(2): 152–172.

Biesta, G. (2011). Combining methodologies. In J. Arthur, M. Waring, R. Coe and L. Hedges (Eds) *Research methodologies and methods in education* (pp. 179–190). London: Sage.

Black-Hawkins, C. (2008). A review of previous studies of researching networks. In C. McLaughlin, K. Black-Hawkins and D. McIntyre (Eds) *Networking practitioner research*. London: Routledge, Ch. 6.

Burke, C. (2007). The view of the child: Releasing 'visual voices' in the design of learning environments. *Discourse, 28*(3): 359–372.

Campbell, C. and Sherington, G. (2006). *The comprehensive public high school*. New York: Palgrave Macmillan.

Cooperrider, D., Whitney, D. and Stavros, J. (2008). *Appreciate inquiry handbook: For leaders of change*. Brunswick: Crown Custom.

Dowling, A. (2007). *Australia's school funding system. A policy brief.* Hawthorn, Victoria: Australian Council for Educational Research.

Dressman, M. (2008). *Using social theory in educational research*. New York: Routledge.

Eagleton, T. (1996). *The illusions of postmodernism*. Oxford: Blackwell.

Fals Borda, O. (2000). People's space times in global processes. The response of the local. *Journal of World Systems Research, 6*(3) Fall/Winter 2000, pp. 624–634.

Fielding, M., Bragg, S., Craig, J., Cunningham, I., Eraut, M. Gillinson, S., Horne, M., Robinson, C. and Thorp, J. (2005). *Factors influencing the transfer of good practice*. DES Research Report RR 615. University of Sussex.

Fielding, M. and Moss, P. (2011). *Radical education and the common school: A democratic alternative*. London: Routledge.

Groundwater-Smith, S. and Mockler, N. (2002). *Building knowledge, building profession-alism*. Paper presented to the Annual Conference of the Australian Association for Research in Education. University of Queensland, December.

Groundwater-Smith, S. and Mockler, N. (2003). *Learning to listen: Listening to learn*. Sydney: University of Sydney Faculty of Education & Social Work/MLC School.

Groundwater-Smith, S. and Rubbo, A. (2010). *Redesigning the school environment: Students as clients*. Presentation at the Symposium Consulting Young People, Why Student Voice Matters convened at the AARE Annual Conference. Melbourne, 28 November–2 December.

Groundwater-Smith, S., Martin, A., Hayes, M., Herrett, M., Layhe, K., Layman, A. and Saurine, J. (2006). *What counts as evidence: Mixed methods in a single case*. Paper presented at the AARE Annual Conference. Adelaide, November.

Kelly, L. and Groundwater-Smith, S. (2009). Revisioning the physical and on-line museum. *Journal of Museum Education, 34*(4): 55–68.

Kemmis, S. (2011). A self-reflective practitioner and a new definitive of critical participatory action research. In N. Mockler and J. Sachs *Rethinking educational practice through reflexive inquiry* (pp. 11–30). Rotterdam: Springer.

Kemmis, S. and Smith, T. (2008). Personal praxis: Learning through experience. In S. Kemmis and T. Smith (Eds) *Enabling praxis: Challenges for education* (pp. 15–37). Rotterdam: Sense Publishers.

Lawson, H. (2001). Active citizenship in schools and the community. *The Curriculum Journal, 12*(2): 163–178.

Mitchell, C., Weber, S. and Yoshida, R. (2008) Where are the youth? Reframing teacher education within the context of youth participation. In A. and J. Sumsion (Eds) *Critical readings in teacher education: Provoking absences* (p. 139). Rotterdam: Sense.

Mockler, N. and Groundwater-Smith, S. (2011). Weaving the web of professional practice: The Coalition of Knowledge Building Schools. In B. Lingard, P. Thomson and T. Wrigley (Eds) *Changing schools: Alternative models* (pp. 294–322). London: Routledge.

Needham, K. (2005). *Zen and the art of school improvement: A case study of using students as researchers into their own learning.* Paper presented to the joint Collaborative Action Research Network/Practitioner Research Conference. Utrecht, November.

Needham, K. (2011). Professional learning in an Across School Network. In N. Mockler and J. Sachs *Rethinking educational practice through reflexive inquiry* (pp. 197–212). Rotterdam: Springer.

Needham, K. and Groundwater-Smith, S. (2003). *Using student voice to inform school improvement.* Paper presented to the International Congress for School Effectiveness and Improvement. Sydney, January.

Sachs, J. (2011). Skilling or emancipating? Metaphors for continuing teacher professional development. In N. Mockler and J. Sachs (Eds) *Rethinking educational practice through reflexive inquiry* (pp. 53–168). Rotterdam: Springer.

Schatzki, T. (2002). *The site of the social.* Pennsylvania: Pennsylvania University Press.

Schatzki, T. (2005). Peripheral vision: The sites of organizations. *Organization Studies,* 26: 465–484.

Wenger, E. (1998). *Communities of practice: Learning, meaning and identity.* Cambridge: Cambridge University Press.

Wilkinson, I., Caldwell, B., Selleck, R., Harris, J. and Dettman, P. (2007). *A history of state aid to non-government schools in Australia.* Canberra: Department of Education, Science and Training.

Chapter 7

Constructing transformative professional knowledge

Having documented in the preceding chapters a variety of perspectives in relation to transformative facilitation, illustrated by a number of cases, we now ask ourselves what kinds of knowledge are being produced in relation to underlying theoretical premises and specific processes. Thus in this chapter we focus upon the nature of professional knowledge that is co-constructed within a transformational partnership and is knowledge for all who are involved in the interactions. We are mindful that there can and should be a legacy of practice-based professional knowledge that remains after individual facilitated projects have been completed. We see that it is possible to develop knowledge through a series of what Stake (2010: 198) refers to as 'petite generalisations', growing what we might call a wisdom of practice that contains a substantial moral and ethical dimension, furthering our claim that the work in which we are interested transcends the kind of facilitation that limits itself to the transactional. We take cognisance of the notion of the knowledge itself gathering in a circular form, rather than as a series of facts heaped upon facts. We see the resultant knowledge as informed descriptions *of* practice rather than prescriptions *for* practice.

At the very heart of our work is the belief, as outlined in Chapters 1 and 2, that facilitation rests upon substantive claims with their appeal to ethical norms and moral judgement as opposed to instrumental and bureaucratised procedures serving what are essentially unquestioned pragmatic purposes. The knowledge that is produced under these conditions is a more profound knowledge of praxis and of the multiple routes towards the resolution of complex dilemmas. Furthermore, in Chapter 3 we have demonstrated how critical it is that we have knowledge of political contexts and their effect, paying particular attention to a knowledge of consequences of the hegemonic dominance of neo-liberal policies. For we well understand that the various facilitation processes with which we are concerned are acted out within an increasingly globalised educational environment that finds itself dominated by an economic rationality that eschews professional activism aimed at developing an informed and critically aware teaching force in favour of one that is designed to serve the often narrow instrumental purposes of government.

Chapter 4 not only focuses upon the ways in which professional knowledge is constructed and nurtured through relationships that are enduring and sustainable, but also brings to the fore questions in relation to theoretical knowledge, characterised as propositional knowledge, and practical understandings seen as familiar, sometimes tacit and based upon experience; matters to which we return at a later point in this chapter. It was argued that teachers developed different kinds of knowledge (Rönnerman, 2005). This knowledge included, for example, forms of personal knowledge that develop through journal writing and personal insights, collegial knowledge that develops through critical dialogue, reflection and meaning making in the group with the facilitator and discursive and communicative knowledge that develops when practitioners talk about their work outside of their own immediate practice. In Chapter 5, knowledge underpinning the facilitation process itself, seen as a 'pedagogy of facilitation', is identified as a significant gap in the literature that attends to the nature of partnerships between the academy and the field. This brings us to the discussion in Chapter 6 regarding the manner whereby communication practices can contribute to knowledge formation. Here we point to the creation of the kind of discursive community that is characterised by clarity and mutual regard. We argue that sound communication is the foundation upon which the specific professional community is grown and developed.

Our concern then in this chapter is to build on these preceding chapters and outline the nature of what we see to be transformative professional knowledge that will enhance and inform practice in ways that are fair, ethical and just, and that are also perceived as legitimate in both the context of the field of practice and academia. We shall discuss the kinds of facilitation that can best help us all, practitioners in universities and schools, create a world that will make a difference for young people, enabling them to grow and learn as able and informed citizens. In her address to the annual conference of the British Educational Research Association, one of the authors of this book, Groundwater-Smith (2007), cited Bertolt Brecht as he sought the answer to Lenin's question 'Wie und was soll man lernen?' (How and what should we learn?) and, of course, 'why?' She argued that academic researchers also need to find some answers to these questions in relation to practitioner research – how and what can we learn from those who investigate their own practice in the field. Why should we seek to learn? Is it, and can it be, truly transformational? Practitioner research requires courage to confront social problems rather than escape them. This is particularly challenging for today's teachers who work within the established order of the various education systems who employ them. It requires rational reflection and critical insight in contexts that are often muddied by short-term policies inspired by political ideology.

We see our first task is to eschew the notion that the knowledge that counts can only be constructed in the academy and then offered to the field of practice. Joram (2007: 124) in discussing what she nominates as 'clashing epistemologies' decries the perspective that believes that: 'University based educational researchers may assume that once their research is carried out they just need to "throw it over the fence" to the eagerly awaiting audience who will then implement the findings.' While this is crudely put, there is no question that the notion that those in the field have neither the insight nor capacity to create substantive professional knowledge, is one that is strongly maintained and argued for in the academy.

Take the work of Labaree (2003), who appears to have some sympathy with teachers as researchers, but who describes the cultural orientation of teachers as normative, personal, particular and experiential, while those in the academic sphere have an orientation to the analytic, intellectual, universal and theoretical. He argues that 'under circumstances of great complexity, vast scale, uncertain purpose and open choice' (p. 14) the capacity of practitioner researchers is one that is constrained by subjectivity (or what Joram 2007: 133 calls 'the cult of the particular') and role definition. For, he argues, the major task of the teacher is to teach and teach well, compared to the academic who is expected to engage in research and scholarship as well as teach their tertiary students. Certainly, he recognises that his own dichotomy is not as clear-cut as it first presents and that, indeed, the academic researcher is also something of a captive of the normative, personal, particular and experiential. However, in part, his argument breaks down in that he bases his case upon the perceived challenge of re-socialising teachers into becoming researchers within doctoral programmes, a matter that appears to be overlooked by many who cite his work. He appears to marginalise, altogether, those who are not in pursuit of a credential, but have an interest in improving practice, often little by little, and with the support of an academic partner who is not a doctoral supervisor with all that entails, but is rather a colleague of equal status. We can read this in contrast to the position taken by Cochran-Smith and Lytle (1999: 262) in their discussion of the essential nature of teacher learning *in situ* where they coined the term 'knowledge *in* practice' to describe 'the emphasis of knowledge *in* action: what every competent teacher knows as it is expressed or embedded in the artistry of practice, in teachers' reflections on practice, in teachers' practical inquiries, and in teachers' narrative accounts'.

We see, in concert with Winter (1998: 374–375) that the process of action research/practitioner inquiry generates its own form of theory:

> This is a form of theory which is integrative, critical and political; it is both personal and collective, a synthesis of values and understandings, and a

response to the many methodological dimensions of practical action in complex organisations profoundly influenced by external political forces.

Thus, in our work we are interested in pursuing the connection between the world of ideas, the analytic, intellectual and theoretical world and the messy world of practice. We argue that the area of shared understanding and experience can be increased by the kind of facilitated practitioner inquiry conducted within transformational partnerships that we set out in our introductory chapter.

Knowledge that enhances professional learning

Fundamental to our argument is that the knowledge that enhances professional learning is produced through four essential social processes, these being the capacity to:

- challenge and support each other's perception of a phenomenon;
- create dialogic conditions that allow varying views and beliefs to emerge and be debated in the understanding that participants are speaking honestly and openly;
- examine such beliefs in the context of the needs and interests of others, especially those who are vulnerable and have little or no voice;
- develop authentic critique that gives expression to legitimate action.

Challenging and supporting perceptions of a phenomenon

In addressing this social process of challenge and support it is worth turning to the work of Bridges (1996), who argues that much of the current press to action research and its relation to the academy is based upon a policy of pragmatism, arguing that 'pragmatism is the banner of common sense' (ibid.: 247). He continues, 'As a theory of knowledge it has demonstrated the roots of knowledge in subjectivity . . . it offers a picture of knowledge which is provisional, functional, and conveniently "self-reparative"' (p. 248). Bridges, however, does not abandon classroom inquiry at this point. He suggests that as an antidote to such pragmatism there can be an abrasion of viewpoints and perspectives that can be both challenging and productive of new knowledge. This is clearly demonstrated in Chapter 2 that reports on the Dutch element of the joint Netherlands, Britain, Russia and United States project, Action Research in Teacher Education (ARTE), where the interaction between the school-based practitioners and university-based facilitators was dialogic rather than instructional with a kind of 'seesawing' between the roles. Thus what evolves can transcend mere opinion. The academic partner, willing to engage with the school-based practitioner with a transformative intention, will look to develop a relationship that is generative in a manner that is reciprocal and respectful. At its best this relationship is one that allows both parties to engage with ideas, beyond the 'what works' solutions, with each having a disposition to: an open and questioning mind; an empathic concern; patience; high expectations of each other; acknowledge different forms of expertise; flexibility and a preparedness to engage in vigorous debate.

Creating dialogic conditions that allow varying views and beliefs to emerge

Powerful professional knowledge does not emerge, unscathed, from single activities or single-mindedness. Carr (2006: 429) asserts that it is through dialogue that participants 'rationally revise their understanding so as to transcend the limitations of what within this tradition has hitherto been said, thought and done'. Were it not so, educational practices would have no possibility of change for the better. As we observed in Chapter 4, establishing relationships that are authentically generative requires time as a component of the infrastructure that governs a given project, time that allows understanding to develop in both breadth and depth. Similarly, the narratives of practice captured in Chapter 6 illustrate the ways in which professional knowledge development accommodates the varying perspectives of those who have a stake in the practice, be they working in school or university contexts.

Examining beliefs in the context of the needs and interests of others

We contend that there was no 'right way' or formula for best practice, for it is never possible to know whether this or that is the 'best thing to do'. 'Best' suggests that a specific solution is irrefutable, but we argue that all solutions are temporary because the social situation is fluid and changeable. What is 'best' is best for the time being within the particular context in which it is enacted.

Rather, we prefer the concept of 'good enough practice'. Taking as a metaphor Winnicott's (1967) concept of 'the good enough mother', 'good enough' can be seen as an antidote to the idea of the 'perfect' as espoused in the 'best practice' argument. We argue that this book is not a 'best practice' manual that assists in the assembly of existing pieces as it might in an engineering or business context, but rather recognises that human relations in education, with all of the attendant complexity, requires a more adaptive and creative orientation producing conditions that are safe enough for practitioners to take risks and explore ideas in the context of the needs and interests of others, rather than to satisfy a government policy or edict. Indeed, it may be seen in the professional learning chapter's case of facilitated professional learning as a part of postgraduate study that the motivation was a heroic one, with a determination to build the kind of professional knowledge that would be relevant to the participating teachers working with students from a refugee background – young people who had faced significant turmoil and travail. The needs and interests of these young people were to be understood in the context in which they and their teachers found themselves. Engaging them in meaningful learning was not a matter of standardisation along a production belt, but a process of devoting careful consideration to what was understood and what was required.

'Good enough' for us applies to practitioner inquiry that is substantial, sustainable, communicative, developmental and ongoing. It takes account of greatly varying contexts in which facilitation by the academy occurs, among them: where academic credentials are involved in the pursuit of postgraduate qualifications; where there is an emphasis upon ongoing and developmental professional learning and where large-scale action learning/action research projects have been established with an expectation that academic partners will play a significant role.

Developing authentic critique that gives expression to legitimate action

This fourth of our fundamental social practices clearly arises from those that preceded it. Developing a critique first and foremost requires us to re-evaluate what we already think we know. Of course re-evaluating existing knowledge is not a recent discovery. We are all inventors of our own professional knowledge, whether as practitioners in the field or academics in universities. The quality of our invention is dependent upon our ability to evaluate the information that is available to us. This view contrasts with one that proposes that knowledge is something fixed, static and to be received and assimilated without any considerable intellectual activity. As Stenhouse (1979) proposed, 'Information is not knowledge until the factor of error in it is appropriately estimated' (Stenhouse, 1983: 141). However, here is the rub; estimating error is not easily undertaken alone – it is something that requires social interaction as ideas are explored and arguments developed and justified.

Orland-Barak (2006) locates such interactions within the context of 'conversations'. In her analysis of a series of monthly conversations, conducted throughout an entire academic year with field-based practitioners and academic researchers, in relation to mentoring processes, she identified three different forms of dialogues that operated within the conversations: 'Convergent dialogues', 'parallel dialogues' and 'divergent dialogues'. Analysis of the content of the conversations revealed that each of these dialogues constituted unique opportunities for participants to co-construct meanings about a different dimension of the practice being investigated with the academic partners. In 'convergent dialogues' participants mediated together their understandings that converged into learning about possible solutions to a particular dilemma in the practice. 'Divergent dialogues' featured participants' use of the conversation space to depart from their personal contexts of the practice in order to explore, compare and make connections across practices so that participants shifted the focus of the conversation to issues outside their specific contexts. In 'parallel dialogues', participants used the conversation space as a setting for developing their own ideas in a kind of 'dialogue with themselves'. The study suggested that the value of professional support frameworks designed around a conversation component lies both in its potential for creating different and varied kinds of dialogues and to allow the emergence of an authentic critique. Furthermore, as we have argued in the preceding chapter, such dialogue itself can and should be published and made available for continuing analysis and discussion.

Besides a concern to understand the social processes required for the co-construction of professional knowledge, we also argue that it is important to locate and understand something of the knowledge interests that are being served.

Knowledge interests as a framework for professional knowledge construction

While much of what we wish to discuss here draws upon the conceptual apparatus designed by Jurgen Habermas, we do not aspire to use his theories as anything other than a touchstone for organising our thinking on the different knowledge interests that may be served by facilitated practitioner inquiry. Suffice to say, we draw upon a form of social explanation that is pluralistic, bringing the concept of varying knowledge interests together in relation to each other. As Habermas (1984: 3) himself put it: 'Whereas the natural and the cultural or hermeneutic sciences are capable of living in mutually indifferent, albeit more hostile than peaceful coexistence, the social sciences must bear the tension of divergent approaches under one roof'. Too often varying knowledge interests are treated as singular, with no bearing of one upon another. What we wish to explore here is the notion that what are ordinarily defined as three distinctive knowledge interests: technical, practical and emancipatory, are interrelated, while certainly satisfying specific functions. We argue that in identifying the knowledge interest to be served there must be a marriage between 'tools' that are adopted and the purposes for which they are to be put. We take it that when working alongside practitioners in the field it is important that the kinds of knowledge interests being served are made explicit and the inquiry procedures that are adopted are appropriate and understood. Thus we shall take each one and briefly set it in a specific inquiry context.

Technical knowledge interests

Here we find the control and manipulation of practice as a form of instrumental or strategic action. For example, a school engaged in significant structural change that unsettles former processes and procedures may be concerned about the sense of collective efficacy among the staff. Using an established measure, the school might 'take its own temperature' over a series of occasions to see whether there is a growing stability or whether the staff is fracturing in its sense of collective purpose. Of course, if this were the only way in which the issue were to be investigated one might have a concern; but as a legitimate inquiry tool, using a well-developed procedure can be seen to fulfil the need to understand the impact of events upon the nature of teachers' working environment in which there is a core of shared beliefs and understandings of practice. In effect the early reconnaissance of a specific context that will enable concerns and differences to emerge can well be undertaken using technical procedures – we do not eschew them because they are technical, but rather encourage the employment of them as a stepping-stone to move towards a more interpretive mode.

Practical knowledge interests

The investment in practical knowledge interests is an investment in understanding through interpretation of the meanings that the participants give to the situation. Thus as a complement to the use of surveys, such as cited above, it may be the case that those engaged in practitioner inquiry into a large school change might wish to work with colleagues to investigate how and why people are feeling as they do and what the consequences might be. One can presume an inclusive, critical conversation being used in a co-operative attempt to reach an understanding of a matter of shared concern regarding staff adaptation to new and changing circumstances.

Emancipatory knowledge interests

Serving emancipatory knowledge interests takes inquiry into the kind of knowledge that is gained through a form of ideology critique with an intention to transform and enhance the conditions of practice. Again, taking our example from above, it may involve participants in engaging in sustained reflective inquiry that liberates participants from the constraints of 'what is' to the possibilities of 'what might be'. Thus professional knowledge transcends the external world and inhabits the internal communicative space.

Summing up these various trajectories, Kemmis (2010: 12) observes:

Different general approaches to research take different kinds of relationships with praxis. Empirical-analytic research adopts a third-person relationship with practice as an object of enquiry; interpretive-hermeneutic research adopts a second-person relationship with practice as the action of another person who is a subject like oneself; and critical-emancipatory research adopts a first-person relationship with practice as constituted in one's own action or in one's participation in the social praxis of a community or group or profession.

Having the support of an academic facilitator is necessary, but not sufficient, for the fulfilment of each of these knowledge interests. For it is in the ongoing dialogue and debate between the facilitator and the practitioners that each interest is satisfied.

Relationships in practice

Whereas Kemmis speaks to the nature of the relationships *with* praxis, we wish now to examine relationships *within* the practice of facilitated inquiry. We have reiterated a number of times how essential it is that relationships are developed that are mutually respectful and enabling. Such relationships do not come about by chance. In establishing a partnership that has the capacity to be transformational for all actors it is required that the grounds upon which the partnership is being established are made explicit. As Gore and Gitlin (2004) have made clear and as we discussed in our introductory chapter, there does exist a divide in terms of the perceived power and knowledge that are exercised by the different parties. In effect what is needed is a kind of understanding of the different and often volatile cultural conditions and traditions that each experiences in their particular workplace. Many academic partners have come initially from the school sector; however, with the effects of rapid change in its many guises it may be argued that the field they enter as academic partner bears little resemblance to the one in which they formerly operated as teacher. Teachers' work has greatly intensified; the degrees of freedom available to them have been significantly reduced as the global educational environment becomes increasingly competitive and controlled by government policies designed to gain an ascendancy on the educational ladder. As outlined in Chapter 3 accountability mechanisms have encroached on professional autonomy in ways hitherto unimagined. Intensification impacts on professional knowledge building in schools in ways that may not be immediately apparent but nonetheless can inhibit development. In the busy life of the school the focus may be more on 'doing teaching' rather than making explicit the associated pedagogical reasoning (Ballet, Kelchtermans and Loughran, 2006). However, as Mitchell (2002: 264) has noted:

if we wish to promote an education culture where teachers are more aware of, and articulate about, their professional knowledge, and where they regularly reflect on, refine and extend their professional knowledge, then we need to know more about how teachers build and store professional knowledge in the complex world of classroom practice.

We need to know how teachers effectively become knowledge workers.

In turn, change in the academic environment is also one that can constrain and impinge upon partnership practices. The rewards for supporting colleagues in schools are limited and limiting. Quality audits of various kinds seem designed to further increase the separation of academia and the professional field; a matter of real concern when we consider the work of professional faculties. One only has to examine the poignant account rendered by Jones and Stanley (2010), who outline the many challenges and dilemmas facing them when undertaking, in a culture of performativity, what had purported to be a collaborative action research project only to be thwarted by forms of filtering, under-reporting (not being sufficiently celebratory) and censorship exercised by both local authorities and their own university's research culture. They concluded by citing the wicked problem of undertaking a 'complicated navigation process through a web of conflicting obligation'.

This complexity is further compounded when we consider that in school-based settings the relationships within practice are not only between the academic partners but also with the students themselves and even the wider community. So that while Edward-Groves, Brennan-Kemmis, Hardy and Ponte (2010) are quite properly concerned with moral and ethical relationships with students, they also see that they are equally essential with respect to the wider communities and societies in which all the parties live.

> The examination of educational practices *in practice* (presented in this paper) show that in ordinary, everyday actions in schools and classrooms, teacher agency gets diminished when insufficient attention is given to people and their *relationships*, severely constraining educator's scope of action. It is in these relationships and interactions that praxis as 'right moral and ethical conduct' is *practised, developed* and *made visible,* and in which teachers form a reflexive self-understanding of their role in creating the possibilities for right conduct by their students in relation to one another, and in the wider communities and societies in which they live. These relatings are the *living practices* of education.
> (Edward-Groves, Brennan-Kemmis, Hardy and Ponte, 2010: 50)

The facilitation of practitioner research partnerships between schools and universities is dependent upon good relationships between people. These relationships both shape and reflect the particular micro- and macropolitics of the school and university contexts. It is through the 'shaping' of our practice, that we endeavour to engage in the transformative co-construction of professional knowledge that will inform curriculum and pedagogy in school and university settings.

The wisdom of practice

Much of the substance of this book has been taken up with detailed issues regarding the nature of the knowledge that is generated as field-based practitioners (in some cases assisted by their students) and university partners struggle with concepts surrounding professional practice as a form of social responsibility conducted within varying and complex contexts to meet individual and community needs for sustainable improvements in young people's lives. We believe that what is of importance is not only knowledge leading to practical action, but also the knowledge that underpins the judgements that impel that action.

We see that the range of knowledges includes propositional knowledge, knowledge of specifics and strategic knowledge. Consistent with our earlier discussion and arguments we see the centrality of the knowledge of moral and ethical matters and their impact upon learning – learning of students, learning of teachers, learning of academic partners – what might be termed 'discerning knowledge' (Phelan, 2005). Whereas the traditional view holds that 'schools have historically been situated as consumers of knowledge' (Bigum and Rowan, 2009: 135) we have detailed the ways in which facilitated practitioner research that is truly transformative can reveal a store of practical wisdom regarding learning and teaching, content and pedagogy and the conditions under which these are enacted.

The framework presented in Table 7.1 has been used as an organiser. The framework provides a summary and illustration of the key concepts that informed and then connected each chapter. Each chapter illustrates knowledge that both shapes the facilitation of practitioner research and emerges through the facilitation process.

Table 7.1 Critical issues for facilitating practitioner research partnerships

Perspectives	Relationships	Facilitation	Knowledge construction	Dilemmas and challenges
Substance	Understanding relationships between practice and theory and how they underpin substantive knowledge	Utilising processes that enable articulation of knowledge and purposeful connections between theory and practice	Building knowledge embedded in practice and derived from practitioner research Understanding the dynamic by which knowledge informs practice	Taking knowledge to the wider public Using practice-based knowledge to inform theory
Political and cultural context	Understanding relationships between policy and practice, and between ideological, institutional and political positions	Negotiating macro- and micropolitics	Identifying what constitutes transformational knowledge	Reconciling differing political and ideological perspectives
Sustainability	Establishing relationships between partners over time	Fostering practitioner research in ways that have long-term impact	Building knowledge over time and applying knowledge across contexts	Securing commitment and resourcing that enables sustainability
Professional development and learning	Articulating professional learning roles and areas of expertise within partnerships	Identifying facilitation practices that support practitioner research for professional learning	Understanding practitioner research as form of professional learning and knowledge building	Making visible the links between facilitation, professional learning and practice
Communicability	Attending to lines of communication and degrees of shared understanding. Reciprocity in relationships	Developing communicative methods for facilitating partnerships and practitioner research	Devising and utilising tools for making research public across institutional divides	Building a common language for all partners

Conclusion

In sum, when we write of professional knowledge formation in the context of facilitated practitioner research, within transformative partnerships, we are concerned to emphasise that the knowledge is not exclusively for the individual practitioner, but is developed within a professional community of practice. It is knowledge that arises from participation in practice; from knowing how, knowing what and knowing why (including means and ends). Returning to the work by Kemmis (2008) discussed in the opening chapter, where he elaborates on the notion of practice architectures that enable and constrain conduct in three dimensions, he names the 'sayings', 'doings' and 'relatings' of practice. We have used this powerful metaphor throughout our discussion, in particular in Chapter 5 and we see that attention needs to be paid to all three; in particular to the relatings that refers both to participants relating to one another as well as to objects such as resources, materials, products and artefacts.

We see that a function of partnerships is to move beyond the celebratory (Groundwater-Smith and Mockler, 2009) and should provide opportunities to marry the practical with the imagined worlds in ways that are critical and enlightening. We believe that practice, whether in the academy or the field, requires the guidance of a moral compass that provides the interpretative structure that gives purpose to our actions.

At the beginning of this chapter we placed an emphasis upon interpretation and the development of meaning, always within the constraints of the language of the possible. We understand the possibilities of knowledge creation that occurs in the context of transformational partnerships, collaborative and generative relationships between practitioners working across school and university contexts, to far transcend what is possible for isolated individuals, and throughout this chapter we have argued for the importance of forming and sustaining such relationships in the interests of knowledge creation. We now turn, in the final chapter of this book, to consider issues of substance and transformative facilitation.

References

Ballet, K., Kelchtermans, G. and Loughran, J. (2006). Beyond intensification towards a scholarship of practice: Analysing changes in teachers' work lives. *Teachers and Teaching*, *12*(2): 209–229.

Bigum, C. and Rowan (2009) Renegotiating knowledge relationships in schools. In S. Noffke and B. Somekh (Eds) *The Sage handbook of educational action research* (pp. 131–141). Los Angeles: Sage Publications.

Bridges, D. (1996) School-based teacher education: A poverty of pragmatism. In R. McBride (Ed.) *Teacher education policy: Some issues arising from research and practice*. London: Falmer Press, pp. 247–256.

Carr, W. (2006). Philosophy, methodology and action research. *Journal of Philosophy and Education*, *40*(2): 421–437.

Cochran-Smith, M. and Lytle, S. (1999). Relationships of knowledge and practice: Teacher learning in communities. *Review of Research in Education, 24*: 249–306.

Edward-Groves, C., Brennan-Kemmis, R., Hardy, I. and Ponte, P. (2010). Relational architectures: Recovering solidarity and agency as living practices in education. *Pedagogy, Culture and Society, 18*(1): 43–54.

Foray, D. and Hargreaves, D. (2003). The production of knowledge in different sectors: A model and some hypotheses. *London Review of Education, 1*: 7–19.

Gore, J. and Gitlin, A. (2004). [Re]visioning the academic-teacher divide: Power and knowledge in the educational community. *Teachers and Teaching: Theory and Practice, 10*: 35–58.

Groundwater-Smith, S. (2007) *Today's children of Mother Courage. What can we learn from them?* Keynote address BERA Annual Conference. London 5th–8th September.

Groundwater-Smith, S. and Mockler (2009) *Teacher professional learning in an age of compliance*. Rotterdam: Springer.

Habermas, J. (1984). *Theory of communicative action, Volume 1: Reason and the rationalisation of society*. T. McCarthy, Trans. Boston: Beacon.

Jones, M. and Stanley, G. (2010). Collaborative action research: A democratic undertaking or a web of collusion and compliance. *International Journal of Research and Method in Education, 33*(2): 151–163.

Joram, E. (2007). Clashing epistemologies: Aspiring teachers; practicing teachers' and professors' beliefs about knowledge and research in education. *Teaching and Teacher Education, 23*: 123–135.

Kemmis, S. (2008). *Practice and practice architectures in mathematics education*. Keynote address to the 31st Annual Mathematics Education Research Group of Australasia (MERGA) Conference. University of Queensland. Brisbane (St Lucia) 28 June–1 July.

Kemmis, S. (2010). Research for praxis: Knowing, doing. *Pedagogy, Culture and Society, 18*(1): 9–27.

Labaree, D. (2003). The peculiar problem of preparing educational researchers. *Educational Researcher, 32*, 13–22 May.

Mitchell, J. (2002). Learning from teacher research for teacher research. In J. Loughran, I. Mitchell and J. Mitchell (Eds) *Learning from teacher research* (pp. 249–266). New York: Teachers College Press.

Orland-Barak, L. (2006). Convergent, divergent and parallel dialogues: Knowledge construction in professional conversations. *Teachers & Teaching, 12*(1): 13–31.

Phelan, A. (2005). On discernment: The wisdom of practice and the practice of wisdom. In G. Hoban (Ed.) *The missing links in teacher education design: Developing a multi-linked conceptual framework*. Rotterdam: Springer, pp. 57–74.

Rönnerman, K. (2005). Participant knowledge and the meeting of practitioners and researchers. *Pedagogy, Culture and Society, 13*(3): 291–311.

Stake, R. (2010). *Qualitative research: Studying how things work*. New York: Guilford Press.

Stenhouse, L. (1979). Research as a basis for teaching. Inaugural Lecture University of East Anglia. In L. Stenhouse (1983) *Authority, education and emancipation*. London: Heinemann Educational Books.

Winnicott, D. (1967). Mirror role of the mother and family in child development. In P. Lomas (Ed.) *The predicament of the family: A psycho analytic symposium* (pp. 26–33). London: Hogarth Press.

Winter, R. (1998). Managers, spectators and citizens: Where does 'theory' come from in action research? *Educational Action Research, 6*(3): 361–376.

Chapter 8

Facilitation of transformative research partnerships

Bundling concepts, perspectives and experiences

In this final chapter we discuss a core question:

What counts as facilitation of practitioner research within transformative partner-
ships between academia and the field of practice; how it works, why, for whom and to
what end?

This question is explored through the summarising and connecting of different
educational concepts, perspectives and experiences and integrating them into an
overall framework for analysing, critiquing and understanding similar projects.
Our focus will be on issues of substance and transformation.

Introduction

In this final chapter we return to the central question of this book. That question
can be summarised as follows:

> What counts as facilitation of practitioner research within transformative
> partnerships between academia and the field of practice; how it works, why,
> for whom and to what end?

We will take up this question again here by summarising and connecting the
different concepts, perspectives and experiences in the previous chapters and integrating them into an overall framework for analysing, critiquing and understanding
similar projects. Our focus will be on issues of substance and transformation.

The overall framework is the result of what we formulated in Chapter 1 as
the central aim of the book: to develop a form of practical theorising that
allows the emergence of a more nuanced and complex framing of facilitation,
taking it beyond the commonplace understanding of assistance and support
provided by academics to the field. Instead we have argued for the notion

of shared understanding and experience that can be increased by facilitated practitioner research conducted within transformative partnerships. This argument is further elaborated in the chapters that followed, each from a different perspective: substance, politics, sustainability, professional learning and communicability.

To be able to develop our experiences, concepts and perspectives into an overall framework we will first summarise the substantive cohesion between the five perspectives. After that we deal with the first part of our question, i.e. refining what counts as the facilitation of practitioner research within transformative partnerships between the academic field and the field of practice. Subsequently we will explore the second part of the main question of the book: how facilitation works, why, for whom and to what end. We do this by:

- further development of the praxis concept as presented in Chapter 1 into an overall framework;
- using the framework to explore facilitation of practitioner research in transformative partnerships.

The framework is presented in Figure 8.1 and outlined in the subsequent sections. We will finish with a brief reflection on three central challenges for university facilitators when trying to create shared understanding and provide support assistance.

The substantive cohesion between the five perspectives

In Chapter 7, we conclude that what is important is not only knowledge leading to practical action, but also the knowledge that underpins the judgements that impel that action. This means that practice, whether in academia or the field, requires the guidance of a 'compass' that provides the interpretive structure that gives purpose to our research, as well as the ways in which we transform practice.

Substance

In Chapter 2 we refer to substance as one guiding point for the compass. The terms 'substance' and 'substantive' are derived from the Latin '*sub*', which means 'under', and '*stare*', which means 'stand', so substance is 'that which stands under'. Substance in the context of this book refers to the rules of justice that practitioners – whether in academia or the field – are called on to apply, as distinguished from the rules of procedure they are asked to follow. These rules of justice concern not only claims about actions that transform educational practices for the better, but also claims about the value of practioner research itself. Both are morally informed; they are not objective but normative, and they are not accidental but continuously at stake in the work that we think should be done in transformative partnerships. Underpinning the rules of justice are questions pertaining to how substantive claims can be justified and validated and we assume that this must be done through deliberative practical rationality. This standpoint is often based on theories of Habermas (1981, 1984, 1987), which have also been used by Carr and Kemmis (1986, see also Kemmis, 2001) as foundation for participatory action research (PAR). However, we elaborate on their ideas further with Gilabert's (2005a and b, 2006) more substantive model and claim that the main aim of facilitation in transformative partnerships is to create a space for deliberative practical rationality based on fundamental values of justice, equality and solidarity.

Politics

The substantive nature of practitioner research in tranformative partnerships leads naturally to the statement in Chapter 3 that research in transformative part-nerships is itself always embedded in 'nested' political contexts, namely the global education policy context, the context of large-scale funded projects and the local micropolitical context. We did not suggest that each impacts in the same way across different contexts, nor that each impacts in the same way across the course of a project. There are many internal variables that mediate the politics of practi-tioner research and there is also a plethora of external variables that do the same, more or less powerfully, depending on their prevalence in public discourse and the impact of that public discourse on the world of the school or the academic world. We have demonstrated also that the political context within which practi-tioner research is enacted is complex and multilayered. While the role of the facilitator is in some ways shaped by these politics, a key part of the facilitation process is related to anticipating and providing a foil to some of the more unhelpful political pressures: at times this can be about providing a counter-cultural voice or encouraging teachers to pause and ponder the orthodoxies of their community and society in the light of the provision of just education for young people.

Sustainability

In taking account of the political context it is possible to see both practitioners and facilitators as activists, referring to Sachs' notion of activist professionalism (2003). Establishing such professionalism is not a 'quick fix' solution to an isolated problem; rather it refers to a critical stance that is continuously at stake in transformative partnerships. In Chapter 5 we argue that such a stance presupposes sustainability of the work, which in our book refers to a morally just way of acting that is connected to the 'depth', 'length' and 'breadth' of transformative partnerships, and to the way interpersonal professional 'relationships' are established and maintained. 'Depth' refers to partners' increased awareness of, and insight into, what they are aiming for and why by engaging in specific actions for change. 'Length' refers to having sufficient time to develop partnerships and the discussion and reflection required to construct professional knowledge relevant to the practice context rather than implementing a specific ready-made model developed externally by somebody else. 'Breadth' refers to the ways in which the actions and knowledge of practitioners in schools and universities are of importance, not only for their own workplace, but also for their networks and beyond. Finally, sustainable partnerships propose the development of a more equal relationship among all partners by taking up different roles in the course of the collaboration.

Professional learning

The substantive and political nature of transformative research leading to sustained partnerships presupposes considerable professional learning for all partners in ways that transform the teaching practices in schools, as well as the research practices in universities. Alignments between the goals and priorities of all participants, and their respective institutions, are therefore imperative, as we claim in Chapter 5. Thus the facilitation of professional learning involves considerable 'bridging' work (Rust, 2009) that makes connections between different types of research knowledge, methodologies and different aspects of the professional practice of teachers in schools and academics in university faculties. While good relationships between people associated with a sustained facilitation process are crucial, they can only be built over time, and are most productive when they are underpinned by open exchange; common concern related to the nature of teaching and learning in schools and shared institutional understanding associated with the purposes of practitioner research and partnerships as vehicles for professional learning.

Communicability

If the main aim of facilitation in transformative research partnerships is to create a space for deliberative practical rationality based on fundamental values of justice, equality and solidarity; if facilitation is about anticipating and providing a foil to some of the more unhelpful political pressures; if therefore sustained partnerships are needed and if this calls for bridging the worlds of schools and universities, then communicability is crucial. Communicability is described in Chapter 6 as the capacity of all parties to speak with and understand each other. By expecting speakers, within the context of shared inquiry, to reveal their reasoning and the basis for their argument in terms that can be clearly apprehended by listeners, those listeners will be enabled to apply criteria that allow them to determine whether statements are, to the best of their knowledge, true or untrue, right or wrong, appropriate or inappropriate. Thus dissonant views may be expressed and tested and the emerging professional knowledge reconstituted and action reconsidered. Furthermore, it is not sufficient for such debate to only be conducted at the local level, it should also be a debate that can be engaged in widely through publication in traditional channels, as well as new media, and in such a way that the processes and outcomes of practitioner research are made available for authentic critique.

Practitioner research, facilitation and transformative partnerships

Having summarised the substantive cohesion between the five perspectives we can now deal with the first part of the main question for this book, i.e. refining what counts as facilitation of practitioner research within transformative partnerships between academia and the field of practice. We will do this step-by-step, referring to the cases in the previous chapters for illustration.

Practitioner research

Practitioner research in transformative partnerships emerges in the various chapters as collaborative knowledge building by practitioners in the university and the field. It is seen as critical research aiming at emancipatory change via democratic processes of co-constructing knowledge by and for all who are involved in the educational situation to be studied and changed. Moreover – as argued in Chapters 6 and 7 – we are mindful that there can and should be a legacy of practice-based professional knowledge that remains after individual projects have been completed. In the previous chapters we argued more than once that writing for and presenting to the educational world, locally, regionally and globally, is an important aspect of practitioner research. Chapter 5, for instance, showed how students and teacher educators in a university-based course managed to do this.

Practitioner research in partnerships

A key argument in the book, and presented in each chapter, is that partnerships will be best achieved by generating reciprocal understanding through dialogue. Dialogue provides a means to reach equity and solidarity between the different partners. Equity and solidarity are expressed in the mutually supportive relationship between those in the field and those in academia, a relationship leading to the understanding of educational practices on different levels. In the cases we saw that practitioner research in partnerships does indeed have the potential to enable all involved to learn from each other: school students, university students, teachers, school principals, facilitators and/or academic researchers. In several cases learning was also seen beyond the school, for instance at the level of the local authorities. Reciprocal learning was true for the different types of partnerships that were presented, whether they were formal partnerships in university courses (Chapters 4 and 5) or informal partnerships in networks of several schools and university partners (Chapters 2 and 6). In each case it was stressed that such relationships also assume reciprocal understanding of the often disparate worlds of the university and the schools. Understanding of each other's institutional, cultural and political contexts and practices, as described in Chapter 3 and elsewhere in the book, proved to be a difficult yet key aspect of partnerships that aim to develop professional knowledge by transforming practice.

Practitioner research in transformative partnerships

Each chapter has therefore problematised the 'gap' between theory and practice, i.e. the gaps between academia and schools, researchers and teachers, and between research and action in one way or another. Each chapter has also sought to demonstrate ways in which partnerships between schools and universities can help to reduce these gaps. The desire to reduce the gap between theory and practice mirrors our fundamental disagreement with transactional models of knowledge building and changing practice. These models presume a linear progress from research to practice where the research design, development and field-based implementation are driven by expert knowledge that evolves in academia and is then implemented in the field. In education this approach has mainly been directed toward solving practical problems through the development and transfer of instrumental and usable knowledge that is value-free, free therefore from substantive claims and judgements. In transformative partnerships, by contrast, we presume a reciprocal relationship between research and practice, based on ongoing negotiation and renegotiation of substantive claims and judgements by all involved in the research. Hence, participants in the different cases presented in each chapter have negotiated not only what should be done and how, but also why, for whom and to what end. Their work was indeed value-bound – as defined in Chapter 2 – because it was based on a priori claims for social change and because they aimed to actually transform professional practices on the basis of those claims. The case in Chapter 2 showed that the participating teachers gradually developed a more substantive stance on these claims. The case also shows that participants developed this stance alongside a number of 'professional orientations' and with help of a facilitation process that is cyclical, explicit, negotiated, forceful and critical.

Facilitation of practitioner research in transformative partnerships

In all cases the main aim for the facilitation of practitioner research in transformative partnerships pertained to creating the conditions for participation and critical dialogue in order to develop professional knowledge and achieve significant social change. Based on the theories of Habermas (1981, 1984, 1987), we argue in Chapters 2 and 6 that these conditions are needed in order to create a communicative space for justifying the substantive moral – hence normative – claims in practitioner research by deliberative practical rationality. Habermas – as we argue in Chapter 2 – defines this process as an inter-subjective practice in which people select and ground the rules that are given to govern their common life with regard to issues of justice. The norms justified in such practice, as well as their application, are to be determined by argumentative processes in which all concerned can participate. The outcome must be equally in the interest of all (see also Carr and Kemmis, 1986). In all chapters, whether or not explicitly, we recognise the three levels on which normative claims can be made, according to Gilabert (2005a and b, 2006):

- First order: specific ethical norms placing constraints on how to apply basic moral ideas in practice
- Second order: norms determining the practices of decision-making and justification concerning the first order norms
- Third order: basic moral ideas about freedom, equality and solidarity as the foundation for social justice.

From all the cases we learned that relationships aimed at deliberative rationality cannot simply be assumed to be there without the support of the facilitator. This support was – in line with Van Stokkum's theory (2011 – see Chapter 2) – shaped as a form of hospitality, which in essence is about 'sharing a finite space'. As a participant in that space you are a temporary guest and you share that space with others. In all the cases presented, the academic facilitator was host first and took the lead in that space, ensuring that the situation in hand proceeded to a good outcome. As host they introduced asymmetry into the relationships in a way, not to emphasise or perpetuate hierarchical relationships (as in the transactional model), but to make things go smoothly and take responsibility for proper regulation of public deliberation and rational argument about 'what is' and 'what ought to be'. Interestingly this authority was indeed often temporary because other participants took over the role of host. The cases in Chapters 4 and 6 especially demonstrate long-lasting developments in local contexts. In both cases it is interesting how the driving force is taken over by the professionals in schools so that the partnerships continue to be based on their desire, resulting in the extension of their scope for decision-making and actions and a belief in building their work based on the democratic values of social justice, equity and solidarity in their own context.

Further development of and exploration with the praxis concept as presented in Chapter I

So far we have explored what for us counts as facilitation of practitioner research within transformative partnerships between academia and the field of practice. What was hitherto left out was the cultural, political and economic context in which partnerships are established. The interplay with this context – as explored in Chapter 3 – was decisively important for the exploration of the second part of the main question of the book: how facilitation of practitioner research in transformative partnerships works alongside why, for whom and to what end.

To understand the daily practice of such partnerships within current cultural and political contexts, we introduced the concept of praxis as a joint lens through which we addressed the challenges that are faced by practitioners both in universities and schools. The use of this concept is based on the work of Ax and Ponte (2008, see also 2010; Ponte and Ax, 2011) and extended with ideas related to practice architecture borrowed from Kemmis (2008, 2010). Praxis refers to social action (such as facilitation of practitioner research) embedded in social contexts, which can be analysed and criticised in terms of its fundamental norms and values – whether intentional or not – about what is morally just or unjust. Furthermore, we argue in Chapter 1 that praxis can be understood as the interplay between *system* and *life-world* on the one hand, and *functional* and *substantive rationality* on the other hand.

In this section we will further develop this concept by drawing on the concepts, perspectives and experiences in each of the previous chapters. We will first do this analytically by unpacking and extending the individual components in the praxis concept with the help of the cases in the previous chapters.

Unpacking and further development of the praxis concept

In Chapter 3 we argue that facilitating critical research is a political act, in so far as the transformational intent is political, a means by which teachers and researchers might enter into professional renewal, explore and problematise their practice and engage in what we defined above, in line with Sachs (2003), as activist professionalism. Activist professionals, as we argue in Chapter 1, try to use and enlarge their scope for decision-making as well as their scope for action (see also Figure 8.1).

Scope for decision-making

Professionals' scope for decision-making depends on the possibilities they have for *functional rationality* (that is what they say about how to realise values and aims set by others), as well as *substantive rationality* (that is what they say about values and aims). So, when trying to answer the question regarding how facilitation of practitioner research in transformative partnerships works, alongside why, for whom and to what end, we have to explore whether partnerships actually use their scope for substantial decision-making (making decisions about aims and values) or whether their scope for making decisions is limited to more instrumental matters.

Scope for action

Professionals' scope for action, by contrast, concerns the possibilities to actually put professional decisions into practice. Scope for action depends, according to Habermas (1981, 1984, 1987), on the interplay between *system* and *lifeworld*. *Lifeworld* is the domain where people organise their own reality, based on their own preferences and in dialogue with others. *System*, on the other hand, is driven by economic, legal, administrative and bureaucratic subsystems that have self-regulating, anonymous dynamics. Chapter 3 elaborates on the way *lifeworld* in both universities and schools is ruled by these dynamics in nested contexts on three levels of *system*: the local, the regional and national funding regulations and the global. Hence we have added these three levels to the praxis concept as visualised in Figure 8.1.

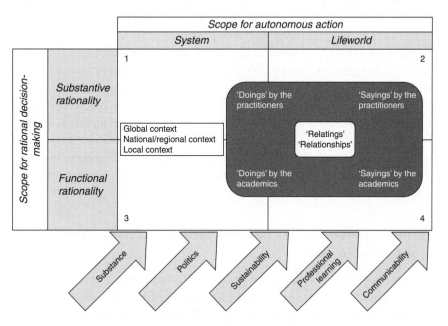

Figure 8.1 Facilitation of practitioner research in transformative partnerships as praxis.

Sayings, doings, relatings and relationships

The interplay between *system* and *lifeworld* on the one hand, and *functional* and *substantive rationality* on the other can be connected to Kemmis' theory of practice architectures (2008, 2010). In the different chapters we have seen how systems provide the mediating preconditions (or meta-practices) for *lifeworld* with 'sayings' (the cultural-discursive dimension), 'doings' (the material-economic dimension) and 'relatings' (the social-political dimension). In line with this, 'sayings', 'doings' and 'relatings' were used in other chapters to denote how the interplay between the four cells manifests itself in *lifeworld*. We recognise, however, a level of ambiguity around the use of the term 'relatings'. It seems that Kemmis (2008, 2010) uses this term for the interconnectedness between material and cultural meta-practices as well as the personal relationships between those involved in those practices. For the purposes of this book we do suggest however an explicit distinction between the two terms, namely 'relatings' between all (meta) practices in which the partners work and 'relationships' among all partners in those practices. With regard to the latter one can easily conclude from the case that nothing would have happened if reciprocal, respectful yet critical relationships between the partners were not established. This is made especially explicit in Chapters 4 and 5. This does not mean that such relationships are simply there. We found throughout the cases that these relationships have to be established among professionals in transformative partnerships; partnerships that rest on substantive claims, that are part of nested political contexts, that are sustained over time, that open up communicative spaces and that make manifest professional learning and knowledge construction. The sayings, doings, relatings and relationships can be seen as an expression or manifestation of what is possible within, and what is actually done in transformative partnerships.

We now can integrate the components of our praxis concept in an overall framework as visualised in Figure 8.1. This framework is not meant to describe 'what is the case' in transformative research partnerships, nor to prescribe 'what ought to be the case'. It is meant as a lens through which facilitation of practitioner research in transformative partnerships can be analysed, problematised and understood.

Further exploration of the interplay between the components in the praxis concept

The sayings, doings, relatings and relationships that were described in each chapter demonstrate ways in which the *lifeworld* of partnerships (cells 2 and 4) is developed in relation to *systems* (cell 1 and cell 3), i.e. ways in which both universities and schools are governed by policies in nested political contexts. Practitioners in universities work within research systems that include national and local funding regulations and global customs that enable and constrain the ways in which partnerships can be facilitated and the types of research that can be conducted. Practitioners in schools are likewise located within regimes that regulate their obligations, time and schedules, as well as national curricula, standardised testing and global comparisons that set the conditions for their participation in partnerships. In Chapter 5, for instance, we conclude that in fact what is needed is a kind of understanding of the different and often volatile cultural conditions and traditions that each partner experiences in particular workplaces.

Activities such as facilitating practitioner research in transformative partnerships are not necessarily on the agenda in neo-liberal times, in which states are establishing regimes that compare systems by testing students' performances and that establish performance-based payment of practitioners in both schools and universities. There is a risk here that *system* (cell 1 and cell 3) will take over the professionals' scope for substantive as well as functional decision-making in *lifeworld* (cell 2 and cell 4), leaving them no other choice than to do what the system expects them to do. The different cases in these chapters show however that there is nevertheless room for a more reciprocal and activist interplay between *system* and *lifeworld* (cells 2 and 4). Throughout the book we have described how practitioners themselves in both schools and universities have had an impact on their institutional practices, very much grounded in their efforts to create communicative spaces for inter-subjective deliberative rationality. Chapter 4, for example, made clear how facilitation between the researcher and the teachers could also be transferred to the level of the local education authorities, by forming a widespread network of schools in the community, in which practitioners in the schools and the local 'quality co-ordinator' hosted the facilitation process of practitioner research. We could say that in this case the local authorities took on the role of mediator between *system* at national level and *lifeworld* in schools, establishing a long-lasting relationship between the school, the university and the local authorities.

In the effort to create communicative spaces for inter-subjective deliberative rationality, we saw that reflection on the interplay between *system* and *lifeworld* is not enough to understand professionals' moral decisions about whose interests their actions serve and the purpose of these actions. To pay attention to this important aspect of making decisions in education, the questions of what to do (*functional rationality*) and why (*substantive rationality*) have to be negotiated. The negotiation between the two rationalities is underpinned by values both in *systems* (cells 1 and 3) and the *lifeworld* (cells 2 and 4). The authors of this book, for instance, represent countries with cultural and political systems built on democratic aims and values upon which their educational systems should be built. These *substantive* aims of *system* (cell 1) can be mirrored in *functional* policies for curricula and syllabi, rules that guide how students should be educated (cell 1). The substantive aims and values and functional means are then in line with basic democratic values such as social justice, equity and solidarity. However, other – more instrumental and industrial – values and means are also present in the current neo-liberal *system*, where economy and competition between individuals and communities are at the forefront. Sometimes there is rhetoric about certain aims at the level of *system* (cell 1), whereas the conditions provided in schools (cell 3) make it impossible to realise those aims.

Moving now to *lifeworld* (cells 2 and 4), rationality is about ways in which practitioners' own values and desires (cell 1) can underline what they are doing in education (cell 4). It is about deciding to be socially just and to act accordingly in spite of the prevailing neo-liberal winds represented in the current system (cells 1 and 3). In *lifeworld* we see how practitioners struggle with national curricula, national testing, grading, inspections and similar matters where someone else is in charge. Out of this national agenda, methods emerge directly or indirectly that practitioners are supposed to use in order to achieve good results according to the national goals and testing instruments. Nevertheless we have seen in the previous examples of how practitioners in the *lifeworld* of schools and universities were trying to move their work beyond the local, regional or national parameters. In Chapter 2 facilitation was shown to be successful by encouraging the participants in the ARTE project to leave their own instrumental thinking and actions within the confines of the well-trodden path and step out deliberately in a new direction. In Chapter 3 we saw that practitioners were able to create a situation in a nationally funded project in which they met external requirements (cell 1 and cell 3) and yet fashioned an approach where local priorities could be addressed. Chapters 4 and 5 give examples of where traditional university classes were transformed into sustainable partnerships. In Chapter 6 we find examples of how universities and schools set up alternative structures for collaboration: practitioners from schools were invited to participate in a coalition of knowledge-building schools while the academic practitioners acted as hosts. The projects carried out in this coalition led to significant change in their own practice and beyond according to the participants.

Challenges for facilitation of practitioner research in transformative partnerships

Through exploring the facilitation of practitioner research in transformative partnerships as praxis, it became obvious that the distinctions between its components can only be made analytically, and at the same time it became clear how much these components of facilitation are dependent on each other in understanding transformational praxis as social action. The interplay turned out to be complex and dynamic and in a way we can talk about two sides of a coin, or better four sides of a cube, where the professional scope for decision-making and action for both academics and practitioners is dependent on all the components in

Figure 8.1. The complexities and dynamics give us reason to finish with some challenges that emerged from our analyses. Our main premise is that the aim of transformative partnerships is to create a communicative space for deliberative rationality and emancipatory change.

Summoning the courage for explicit moral positions

Gilabert (2005a and b, 2006), as described in Chapter 2, argues that when we engage in a process of inter-subjective deliberation in order to justify our moral claims we do indeed endorse the 'Project of Justice'. By engaging in the facilitation of practitioner research in transformative partnerships, we are agreeing that we should try, to the extent that we can, to construct praxis in which all include each other and themselves, in solidarity, as free and equals. This agreement does not, however, constitute a rational ground; it refers to intuitive or intentional grounds for inter-subjective deliberation in the sense that they are explicit moral positions. In other words, if we commit ourselves to facilitating practitioner research in transformative partnerships, we are already expressing a commitment to democratic values of equity, freedom and solidarity. In philosophical terms this might be the case but it is questionable whether this is the case in practice. For instance, when teachers enter a university course (as described in Chapters 4 and 5), they are often simply confronted with the way teacher eductors think courses should be set up. Thus for their facilitation to be successful, facilitators need to clarify their substantive motives for doing things differently in order to avoid ending up with unintended instrumental applications of practitioner research. Yet this is not something that can be done as a kind of announcement beforehand. It is something that should be discussed, shaped and agreed on during the work that is done in partnerships, openly, reciprocally, respectfully and critically. The challenge for facilitators and practitioners both in university and schools is then to summon up sufficient courage to explicitly express substantive issues in a neoliberal age in which – as Susan Neiman (2008, see also Chapter 2) argued – moral claims make many feel profoundly uncomfortable.

Summoning the courage to embrace unhappy stories

A process of intersubjective deliberation assumes, according to Gilibert (2005a and b, 2006), not only endorsing the 'Project of Justice', but simultaneously accepting the 'Fact of Widespread Moral Disagreement'. In other words, by engaging in practitioner research in transformative partnerships we already recognise that we do not immediately agree on our interpretations of what the basic ideas of solidarity, equality and freedom demand from us in different facilitation and research contexts. This means in the first place that partners should be open to critique. Communication in partnerships, as emphasised in Chapters 6 and 7, is not about noncommittal exchange. What evolves should transcend mere experience and opinion. The facilitator therefore leads the challenge to create a situation in which participants dare to question each other critically about their basic values, as well as about how these values are expressed in practice: the practice of deliberative procedures occurs within the partnership as well as the practice of educational transformation. Sustained relationships between all participants of the partnerships are crucial to this, as asserted in Chapter 4, but sustained relationships are constantly in danger of losing their critical function. This happens when from the three aforementioned parameters of sustainability attention is only given to 'length' and 'breadth'. The facilitator should also encourage 'depth' in the communication by encouraging participants not only to celebrate 'happy stories', but also and especially to summon up courage to embrace the unhappy ones and to learn from them. So both the endorsing of the 'Project of Justice' and the 'Fact of Widespread Moral Disagreement' are sources for professional knowledge building and social change. This not only applies within the partnerships themselves, it also applies to publishing the research outcomes in ways that can be scrutinised by educational communities as the local, regional/national and international levels (see Chapters 5 and 6). If that is the assumption, we also need to look at the stories collaboratively – from both the perspectives of the schools and the universities – and to resist the honest stories being judged by the academic world simply as non-research.

Summoning the courage to leave well-trodden paths

Endorsing the 'Project of Justice' and accepting the 'Fact of Widespread Moral Disagreement' in *lifeworld* of partnerships is not only a source of professional knowledge building but simultaneously a source of social change. As the French philosopher Debord (2004) stressed, only 'direct action in daily life' gives rise to the transformation of what he calls the society of the spectacle, in which everything turns on moving from one experience to another, driven by consumerism and media, all strictly in the service of economic interests. Education too is shaped more and more as a spectacle, where teachers and students are introduced to the things to do, preferably as a 'quick fix' in the function of the labour market. If therefore practitioner research in partnerships aims to give rise to Debord's 'direct action in daily life', and if the aim is to transform education into an endeavour that is also focused on 'things to critically think about in human life' then this implies activist professionalism for practitioners both in universities and in schools. In her comprehensive publication about activist professionalism, Sachs (2003) shows that the main challenge is to have the courage to leave well-trodden paths. The cases presented in this book are not therefore concerned with routine choices made by teachers and academics. Rather the cases are about challenging *system* by providing a foil to some of the more unhelpful political pressures in nationally funded projects (Chapter 3) or offering students or teachers 'other things' than ordinary classes, including participation in research projects (Chapter 2), starting courses or professional development as partnerships (Chapters 4 and 5) or initiating networks or coalitions with schools (Chapter 6). These are all examples of how professionals can enlarge the scope for decision-making and action by working collaboratively with other partners. In doing so, it seems that there is some space to challenge *system* and thereby to open up to alternative perspectives and activities in *lifeworld*. Berg (2007) names this space a 'free room'. The model developed by Berg (2003) analyses the outer and inner borders for development in schools. The outer border marks the societal system in the form of politics and rules for education, while the inner border is constituted by the cultures within the institutions themselves, which in turn are built upon history and traditions and thereby become part of *system*. The task for a school or a university is to discover and capture their free room and use it to develop what we called their scope for decision-making and action. Applied to facilitating practitioner research in transformative partnerships it could be about daring to do something other than what one is expected to do by using this free room. Instead of offering practitioners a standard course, for instance, or falling into the trap identified by Carr and Kemmis in which action research becomes 'transformed into little more than a research method that could be readily assimilated to and accommodated within the broader requirements of the orthodox research paradigms' (Carr and Kemmis, 2005: 351). Facilitation is about constructing courses, programmes or networks that can lead to partnerships with the aim of establishing democratic practices for universities and schools, for academics and teachers and in the end, of course, for students. Such facilitation requires taking into account matters of substance, politics, sustainability, professional learning and communicability.

The outcomes of the facilitation of practitioner research partnerships are not possible when we limit our focus to purely practical change. The motive for this book was therefore to integrate the practical focus with an understanding of where the concepts we use, the perspectives we share, and the experiences we endure, are coming from. Critically exploring their philosophical, sociological and historical foundations is therefore inherent to the transformation of educational praxis for the better. In that sense, according to Debord (2004), there is no distinction between theory and life.

References

Ax, J. and Ponte, P. (2008). Praxis: Analysis of theory and practice. In J. Ax and P. Ponte (Eds) *Critiquing praxis* (pp. 1–20). Rotterdam: Sense Publishers.

Ax, J. and Ponte, P. (2010). Moral issues in educational praxis: A perspective from pedagogiek and didactiek as human sciences in continental Europe. *Pedagogy, Culture & Society*, *18*(1): 29–42.

Berg, G. (2003). *Att förstå skolan. En teori om skolan som institution och skolor som organisationer.* [To understand school. A theory about school as an institution and schools as organisations.] Lund: Studentlitteratur.

Berg, G. (2007): From structural dilemmas to institutional imperatives: A descriptive theory of the school as an institution and of school organizations, *Journal of Curriculum Studies*, *39*(5): 577–596.

Carr, W. and Kemmis, S. (1986). *Becoming critical: Education, knowledge and action research.* London: Falmer Press.

Carr, W. and Kemmis, S. (2005). Staying critical. *Educational Action Research*, *13*(3): 347–358.

Debord, G. (2004). *The society of the spectacle.* K. Knabb, Trans. London: Rebel Press.

Gilabert, P. (2005a). A substantivist construal of discourse ethics. *International Journal of Philosophical Studies*, *13*(3): 405–437.

Gilabert, P. (2005b). The substantive dimension of deliberative practical rationality. *Philosophy Social Critisisme*, *31*(2): 185–210.

Gilabert, P. (2006). Considerations on the notion of moral validity in the moral theories of Kant and Habermas. *Kant Studien*, *97*: 211–227.

Habermas, J. (1981). *Theorie des kommunikatieven Handelns.* Frankfurt am Main: Suhrkamp Verlag.

Habermas, J. (1984). *Theory of communicative action, Volume 1: Reason and the rationalisation of society.* T. McCarthy, Trans. Boston: Beacon Press.

Habermas, J. (1987). *Theory of communicative action, Volume 2: Lifeworld and system: A critique of functionalist reason.* T. McCarthy, Trans. Boston: Beacon Press.

Kemmis, S. (2001). Exploring the relevance of critical theory for action research: emancipatory action research in the footsteps of Jürgen Habermas. In P. Reason and H. Bradbury *Handbook of action research* (pp. 94–105). London: Sage Publishers.

Kemmis, S. (2008). *Practice and practice architectures in mathematics education.* Keynote address to the 31st Annual Mathematics Education Research Group of Australasia (MERGA) Conference. University of Queensland. Brisbane (St Lucia) 28 June–1July.

Kemmis, S. (2010). Research for praxis: Knowing, doing. *Pedagogy, Culture and Society*, *18*(1): 9–27.

Neiman, S. (2008). *Moral clarity: A guide for grown-up idealists* (1st edition). Orlando: Harcourt.

Ponte, P. and Ax, J. (2011). Inquiry-based professional learning in educational praxis: Knowing why, what and how. In N. Mockler and J. Sachs (Eds) *Rethinking educational practice through reflexive inquiry* (pp. 49–61). Dordrecht: Springer.

Rust, F. (2009). Teacher research and the problem of practice. *Teachers College Record*, *111*(8): 1882–1893.

Sachs, J. (2003). *The activist teaching profession.* Buckingham: Open University Press.

Van Stokkum, B. (2011). Revitalisering van informeel gezag: Gezag en vrijheid verzoend. [Revitalising informal authority: Authority and freedom reconciled.] *Algemeen Nederlands Tijdschrift voor Wijsbegeerte*, *1*(103): 21–35.

Index